BEHOLD THE MAN

JESUS CHRIST AND TRUE MASCULINITY

BEHOLD THE MAN

JESUS CHRIST AND TRUE MASCULINITY

JOHN TRIFFITT
WITH
MARK STIBBE

BEHOLD THE MAN

Published using KWS services: www.kingdomwritingsolutions.org

ISBN: 978-1505408959

Endorsements

What a stimulating read! In this great book we're taken back in time to the first century AD to look at what manhood and masculinity really meant when the Bible was written. It compares what it meant to be a man in Roman culture with the manhood that was presented by Jesus. Seasoned with cracking stories, this well researched and honest book is a must-read for any man who wants their inner and outer worlds to be conformed to the image most likely to release health, happiness and heroism today.

Steve Legg, Sorted Magazine

John Triffitt, with Dr Mark Stibbe's help, has done a fantastic job in writing this book. Its message is very much needed in the Church today. Indeed, if it were to be applied it could revolutionise men's lives! It tackles the subject of manhood and masculinity very thoroughly and will serve as a resource in my library for many years to come. It is also written very well and so is easy to read and comprehend. I highly recommend it for men — and leaders in particular — to use in groups with other men.

Steve Uppal, Senior Pastor, All Nations

I am writing this as a pastor and friend, having had the privilege of knowing John Triffitt for over twenty years, from the time when he, as a young man, surrendered his life to Jesus. I saw Christ's love set John on fire and this fire has never diminished but only burns brighter and brighter, revealing the Life of Christ in him. The Bible calls this "Christ in us the hope of glory," and this is what I see has made John the man he is. John is an example of the kind of man God can use; his kindness, generosity, integrity, purity, faithfulness and willingness to work hard and believe God to prosper everything he does, and not least his love for Paula — his wife — and their beautiful children is an inspiration to encourage anyone to want to read this excellent book. I believe this book will inspire you to rise like John to greater heights.

Robert Maasbach, Senior Pastor, Life Church, Folkestone UK

Contents

Introduction

In *Behold the Man* our aim is to try to describe what an ideal man really looks like. To do that we will propose that Jesus of Nazareth gives us the most compelling portrait of masculinity the world has yet seen. Put simply, we propose that Jesus of Nazareth is the apex and the epitome of functional and healthy manhood and masculinity.

In many ways this is not a new point. What is unique about our proposal is the way in which we argue this case with reference to the Roman context of the New Testament and specifically Roman ideas of masculinity.

We want to suggest that these ideas provide a revealing backdrop for looking at Jesus' masculinity. More specifically, we want to argue that Jesus' masculinity can best be understood when studied against the backdrop of what the Romans considered to be 'the manly man.'

While Jesus was a Jewish not a Roman man, he lived in a country under Roman occupation and influenced by Roman culture. The Roman cultural background for understanding Jesus is therefore important, not least because the earliest Christians confessed Jesus as 'Lord' in a world where that title was used of Caesar.

We want to argue that the Roman world of Jesus' day had some strong views about what it wanted to see when a boy became a man. These clustered around the concept of *virtus* (translated virtue). Roman boys were supposed to grow into men who embodied virtue and to help with that the Emperor was lauded as the apex of virtue. Roman boys were to look up to him as the perfect image of masculinity.

Jesus of Nazareth was educated in this world. While he was

raised according to the customs and traditions of Judaism, the land in which he grew from a boy to a man was occupied by Roman forces and images of the Emperor were visible everywhere. This Emperor was idolised as 'son of God', 'Lord and God', 'Saviour of the World' — titles which would be applied to Jesus.

It is therefore a fascinating exercise to look at the accepted characteristics of Roman virtue and ask, 'does the Jesus whom we read about in the Gospels exhibit these traits?' Does he offer us an abiding image of what it means to be a man? Does the Carpenter provide a more engaging portrait than the Emperor?'

From there we will go on to look at the implications for Christian men today. What models are Christian men using when it comes to the development of their manhood and masculinity? Are we conforming to the 21st century version of the image of Caesar, or are we conforming to the image of Christ?

Before we begin, however, we need to define two important words — *manhood* and *masculinity*.

Throughout our book, *manhood* will be used to denote the internal life of a man — his thoughts, attitudes, values, aspirations, and so forth.

Masculinity will be used to denote the externally observable aspects of a man's life — his tasks, his conduct, his way of living, and so on.

In *Behold the Man*, we argue that Christ trumps Caesar when it comes to modelling both *manhood* (a man's interior life) and *masculinity* (his externally visible conduct).

We want to propose that Jesus provides the finest example of healthy manhood and creative masculinity, not just in the first century, but in the twenty first too.

PART 1:

BIBLICAL MAN

BEHOLD THE MAN

PROLOGUE

John writes: 'I have always been intrigued by issues of manhood, masculinity and manliness. When I was a boy I was captivated by masculine images of strength, prowess, courage, determination, resolve, heroism, achievement, romance, prosperity, influence, beauty and fame. These pictures would often fuel my dreams when imagining how my life would unfold as a man.

However, looking admiringly at images was as far as it went for me. Indeed, I cannot recall a time during my younger years, nor in my late teens, when I reflected critically or at depth on what it really means to be a man.

When I became a Christian, however, all that changed. The images paraded and celebrated by popular culture started to fade into the background. In their place, I began to consider what the Bible had to say on this subject.

In short, I started to ask myself how the Bible would answer the question, 'What constitutes a real man?'

That moment of curiosity formed the genesis of a dissertation at King's College, London, which Mark and I have now adapted into this book.

For me the research I undertook for that was never a purely academic matter. It was far more than that. It formed the Biblical basis for the understanding of my own masculinity and it has been instrumental in my leadership role in a large church, including my involvement in men's ministry.

I hope it proves helpful to you too.'

BEHOLD THE MAN

Chapter 1:

BACK TO THE BIBLE

Today it would not be an overstatement to say that men are experiencing a crisis of self-understanding when it comes to manhood and masculinity. In a world where there are so many competing ideologies and images of manliness, men are trying desperately to come in from a wild sea of confusion and moor themselves to a secure harbour of clarity. That is by no means an easy task. It is one that requires mental agility and heroic resolve.

Part of the problem here has to do with worldview. A worldview is a set of lenses through which we see and understand our world. It is a matrix of presuppositions — prior ways of thinking — which govern how we view ourselves and our lives. It is what gives a sense of order and meaning to our perspective of reality.

Many men wear a pair of *evolutionist* spectacles when they think about manhood. Using these lenses they reason that it is impossible to settle on a final and definitive view of what masculinity looks like because men — and indeed women — are still in a process of evolving.

Other men wear a pair of *deconstructionist* spectacles. Using these lenses they also say that it is impossible to settle on a definitive picture of masculinity, not because men are still in an evolutionary process, but because there is no such thing as a transcendent and absolute idea of manhood.

Still other men wear a pair of feminist spectacles. Using these lenses they come to believe that a definitive picture of masculinity is not worth pursuing because men oppress women. This leads to some men recreating themselves in the image of a woman and feminizing themselves.

For a Christian man caught up in this dizzying vortex of competing ideologies confusion can abound. However, there is thankfully a resource as reliable as the stars to help him navigate through this turbulent ocean. We are referring to the Bible, whose overarching story or 'meta narrative' provides an intellectually coherent view of the world and indeed of manhood and masculinity for the Christian believer.

What does the Bible have to say to men about masculinity? We could answer by saying, 'almost nothing.' In the Bible, God is transcendent to this material universe. He dwells beyond time and space. Furthermore, he transcends gender. While he is known as 'Father' (an obviously masculine term) he is also known to have maternal qualities and is said to love us in a mother-like way (Isaiah 66.13). God therefore contains the very best of what it means to be both masculine and feminine. He transcends gender and therefore, it could be said, has 'almost nothing' to say about authentic masculinity.

We could also argue, however, that the Bible has 'nearly everything' to say about masculinity. This is because it also reveals that God has come to dwell on the earth as a man. When Jesus Christ was born he was born as a baby boy in Bethlehem. He grew up into manhood and was declared to be God's Son at his baptism by John in the River Jordan. He went about helping those in need and was known as a man approved by God (aner in Greek, Acts 2.22). He was also described as a man — sometimes even 'a mere man' — by those he met. In Jesus Christ, God has accordingly lived as a man on the earth. In doing so, God has sanctified manhood and masculinity and given men a picture of what true manliness looks like.

If we take the second view then authentic masculinity can be defined and described, provided we keep our eyes fixed on the one whom the Apostle Paul calls the Last Adam, that is to say, on Jesus Christ. This Last Adam must be our point of reference if we are to embrace God's redemptive image of masculinity. No other model will help us, and this includes especially the First Adam, who lost what it meant to be truly masculine when he rebelled against his Maker's love.

When the First Adam fell, God came looking for him in the Garden of Eden. In Genesis 3.9 we read, 'Then the Lord God called to Adam and said to him, "Where are you?"'

What is at the heart of this question? The first thing to say is that this is not a request for coordinates. Whenever God asks a question in the Bible, it is never for information. The Biblical God is omniscient; he is all-knowing and-all seeing and therefore does not suffer from ignorance. When God calls to Adam, he is not asking him to disclose an unknown location. He is asking Adam to come out of hiding and to bring his shame into the light.

It is here that we begin to uncover the original source of the deterioration and distortion of masculinity. Since the moments described in Genesis 3.9-10, men have not lived with a clear understanding of the distinctive nature of their gender. Instead, the shame brought about by 'man's first disobedience' has infiltrated the human race as a whole. All human beings have fallen into a distorted view of themselves. Since Adam and Eve, everyone has experienced confusion about their gender and worth. Women don't know that they are princesses or what princesses (in the real world) look like. Men don't know that they are princes or what princes (in the real world) look like either.

So what do men do? Living in the legacy of the First Adam, they seek to cloak their shame and they do this by emulating the men they see and admire in popular culture. Taking their eyes off the Creator, they look at creatures instead, which is the essence of idolatry. They look at popular images of manliness in the mass media and then dress themselves up, both internally and externally, to look like them.

This is really what was going on in the Roman world in the time of Jesus. Roman citizens were educated to engage in idolatry and throughout the Empire were taught from a very early age that their

Emperor embodied true *virtus*.

Look at the word 'virtus' here. The first part of it is the Latin word 'vir', from which we get the word 'virile'. It means a man, as distinct from a woman. When Roman citizens looked up to the Emperor in the time of Jesus, they didn't just treat him as divine and look upon him as a god. They also treated him as human and looked upon him as a man — as the man whom real men admired and imitated, as *'the manly man.'*

In the very act of idolizing this image, Roman citizens were perpetuating the deterioration and distortion of masculinity that had been viral since the time of the First Adam. In other words, they were committing idolatry and in the process were recreating themselves in the image of a man (their Caesar) rather than in the image of God (their Creator).

There is a revealing moment in Mark's Gospel when the Pharisees and Herodians send men to Jesus to entrap him. They begin by flattering him and saying that they know that he is a man of integrity. They then ask him a question about taxes. Should they, as devout Jews, pay taxes to a Gentile Emperor?

Jesus is now on the horns of a dilemma. If he says a straight 'yes', then they can accuse him of giving money to ha goyim (the pagans) which rightfully belongs to God. If he says a straight 'no', then they can accuse him of defaulting on his taxes and breaking the civil law. How is Jesus to answer this?

Jesus' is aware straight away of their desire to try and catch him out. So in Mark's account (Mark 12.15-17) he says,

"Bring me a denarius and let me look at it." They brought the coin, and he asked them, "Whose image is this? And whose inscription?"

"Caesar's," they replied.

Then Jesus said to them, "Give back to Caesar what is Caesar's and to God what is God's."

Jesus' answer here involves a comparison between a Roman coin and the human soul. The coin has the image and inscription of the Emperor on it. The soul, on the other hand, has the image and inscription of the Creator on it.

Jesus addresses his accusers and turns the tables on them. Pointing to the coin, he tells them to be good citizens of their country and pay their taxes. Pointing to their souls, he tells them to be good citizens of heaven and pay the right kind of homage to the God in whose image they have been created. Why does he do this? The answer is simple. In pointing to an image engraved on a coin, Jesus' accusers have already broken one of the Ten Commandments. They are giving too much attention to a graven image. Jesus uses the coin which they themselves have brought as their visual aid and effectively tells them to start worshipping God properly.

What a man!

It is our proposal in this book that the Bible is the most illuminating, radical, subversive and transformational text for understanding the contours of the 'manly man.'

Caesar was regarded as the manly man in the Roman world of the earliest church. It was accordingly the responsibility of every Roman male to fashion themselves in the image of Caesar.

But then into that world comes Jesus of Nazareth, the one man in human history in whom the image of God could be seen in all of its pristine, untarnished glory.

Which image are men going to cultivate — the *imago Caesaris* (image of Caesar) or the *imago dei* (the image of God, revealed in Christ)?

And which image are male believers going to reproduce in their lives today?

BEHOLD THE MAN

Chapter 2:

CRISIS IN MASCULINITY

From the dawn of time men have obeyed a primal call to be innovators and pioneers. In the first chapter of the Bible, the author of the Book of Genesis describes the original mandate which God gave to men and women.

God blessed them and said to them, *"Be fruitful and increase in number; fill the earth and subdue it. Rule over the fish in the sea and the birds in the sky and over every living creature that moves on the ground"*

[Genesis 1.28]

Ever since this divine blessing was spoken, men have had within their human DNA a God-given drive to be fruitful, to multiply, to replenish, to subdue and to exercise dominion in the earth.

Deep down in every man there is accordingly a dim and distant presentiment that life is more than just daily drudgery. There is an ancestral call to live heroically, to embrace an adventure, to change the world and to leave a legacy. Although the consequences of Adam's sin have distorted this divinely-implanted call, God's mandate still resounds in every man today. It is this original mandate which has enabled men to reach for the impossible, to fathom the unfathomable and solve the unsolvable. It has compelled men to further the boundaries of aviation, travel, communication, knowledge, science and medicine. It has brought men into positions of leadership which have freed people from slavery, delivered nations from dictatorships, and built bridges of peace between seemingly irreconcilable people, tribes and nations.

Somewhere within his soul every man senses this 'mandate' — that 'man' has a 'date' with a destiny bigger than himself. Those men who have responded to it with an unstoppable determination have gone on to explore uncharted swathes of land, sea and even stars. It has led them to develop vaccinations, inoculations and medicines which have effectively eradicated diseases and have saved countless millions of lives. Without doubt, men have an extraordinary capacity for good.

At the same time, we men undoubtedly have the extraordinary capacity to err. Even in cultures where men's achievements have been rightly praised, men have also exhibited the ability to cross ethical boundaries and do things which are 'not even named among the Gentiles' (1 Corinthians 5.1). Look at UK culture today. One only has to turn to any news channel or flick through the pages of popular newspapers to witness the depths to which men can descend. Betrayal, adultery, murder, genocide, theft, violence, fraud, promiscuity, pornography, greed, alcohol abuse, drug abuse and selfish ambitions — all these are at epidemic levels among men in contemporary society.

Of course some men plead that this is simply the result of feminist 'misandry' — the feminist's hatred of men and the traditional role played by men. In a frantic attempt to evade responsibility, some suggest that this constantly reinforced portrait of despicable men is really the feminist's version of misogyny. In other words, it is all a myth that serves an anti-male, political agenda.

The data, however, does not support this view.

In fact, the data supports the idea that men are in crisis and are too often expressing their confused manhood in a toxic way.

Take the following as examples.

The England and Wales prison population on the 24th October 2014 was 85,720 of 3,924 were women and 81,706 men.

The average prison population has risen by 3.6% each year since 1993, although there has been a slight decrease over the 2012-2013 periods, with over 95% of the prison population being male.

The top four offences resulting in custodial sentences were violence against another person (20,000), drug-related offenses (11,000), sexual offences (10,000), and robbery (just under 10,000).

Forty-five percent of women have experienced some form of domestic violence, sexual assault or stalking, mainly by men.

Around twenty-one percent of girls experience some form of child sexual abuse, again mainly by men.

At least eighty thousand women suffer rape every year.

On average two women a week in England and Wales are killed by a violent partner or ex-partner. This constitutes nearly forty percent of all female homicide victims.

Seventy percent of incidents of domestic violence result in injury, (compared with fifty percent of incidents of acquaintance violence, forty-eight percent of stranger violence and twenty nine percent of mugging).

Around eighty-five percent of forced marriage victims are women and domestic violence is estimated to cost victims, services and the state a total of around twenty three billion pounds a year.

While the contexts for each of these statistics are often complex, they are still alarming enough to justify the claim that many men are living out distorted and indeed dangerous versions of masculinity today.

Men may have had a noble call at the beginning of time, but in these days it seems that many have forgotten their creative mandate and have turned their focus and energy to non-productive and harmful ends.

Men have lost their vision for healthy and functional masculinity. The original image has become marred and disfigured.

Truly, there is a crisis of manhood and masculinity today.

BEHOLD THE MAN

Chapter 3:

THE FADED IMAGE

Christians believe that the Holy Scriptures are God-breathed and contain God's special revelation to mankind. These Scriptures (understood today to refer to both the New Testament as well as the Old) are indispensible for understanding what to believe and how to behave. To use the technical terms, for Christians the Bible has divine authority in matters of orthodoxy (right believing) and orthopraxy (right behaving). This divine authority derives from the fact the Bible has a divine author. It is not a merely human, literary production.

What then does the Bible have to say to the crisis in masculinity?

First of all, there is good news. The good news is that in spite of man's capacity to err, his position in the divine order of things is one of extreme honour and privilege. If we are in any doubt about this we should go to Psalm 8. The psalmist asks, 'What is man that you are mindful of him and the son of man that you visit him?' Notice the masculine language here. While the first word 'man' is inclusive of both genders (as in 'mankind', referring to mortal human beings in general), the phrase 'son of man' is *ben adam* in Hebrew, a male designation.

Now see what the psalmist adds as a qualifier, 'for you have made him a little lower than the angels, and you have crowned him with glory and honour.' Here we should note a common mistranslation in our English Bibles. The New King James Version says that the sons of men are little lower than the angels. This is not what is written in the original Hebrew.

In the original text, the word translated 'angels' is *Elohim*, one of the commonest names for God. Far from saying that the sons of men are just a little lower than the angels, this magnificent psalm extols God for placing the sons of men just a little lower than *Elohim* — than God himself.

This then makes sense of the New Testament teaching that angels are ministering spirits who are sent by God to serve those who are in Christ (Hebrews 1.14). How can these angels serve us if we are lower than them? If however, the sons of men are just a little lower than God that means that they are also higher than the angels. This is indeed a glorious truth — one that should inspire our highest praise. For who among us would ever say that we deserved such an honour? Who among us would ever dare to claim that we are worthy to be crowned with such glory?

At this point we need to ask why men have such a place of honour in the sight of God. The answer has to do with the *forming* of the first man Adam.

In Genesis chapters 1 and 2, we learn two truths that are essential for our understanding of the honour which God gives to men.

The first has to do with the difference between the way God forms the first man and the way he forms everything else. A number of times we read the expression 'and God said' in Genesis chapter 1. After each use of the phrase, something comes into existence: first the light, then the firmament, then the earth and seas, then vegetation, then the sun, moon and stars, then the birds of the air and the fish of the sea, then the land animals. In every case, things are spoken into existence.

In the case of the first man — Adam — there is a big difference. While it is true that God says 'let us make man in our own image,' the actual means of creating the first male are very different from the process used to form the seas, the stars, the sun etc. In the case of Adam (as in the first male, 'Adam'), God did not speak him into existence. God formed him out of the dust of the earth.

While everything else is spoken into being, the first man is formed by the loving hands of Abba, Father. The Hebrew word bara translated 'create' adds a further hint about this singular privilege. It is a verb that has God himself as the subject and man as the object. Furthermore, it is a verb that was often used of a potter forming something out of clay. When God created the first male, he took the dust of the earth and formed something as artistically exquisite as the world's most priceless vase. God moulded Adam with his hands between his thumb and forefinger, with the tender and creative devotion of a sculptor or a potter.

So just in the matter of the *forming* of Adam we can see why he is worthy of a special honour.

A second factor that makes man the focus of honour in the sight of heaven has to do with the *filling* of Adam. In Genesis 2 we read that God fills Adam with his spirit. In verse 7, we see that 'God formed man of the dust of the earth and breathed into his nostrils the breath of life; and man became a living being.' There are accordingly two awe-inspiring moments in the creation of the first man Adam. The first involves God forming the man, as a potter would form a vase out of clay. The second involves God *filling* the man as he breathes into Adam's nostrils the breath of life.

How close did the Father have to be to this newly formed man to breathe into his nostrils?

Close.

Very close.

Face to face, in fact.

This was a moment of unbridled and unprecedented intimacy.

God looked into Adam's face and gently blew his *ruach*, the wind of his breath, into the man's nostrils. And the whole company of heaven was dazzled.

Adam at that moment became something altogether different from every other created thing, whether animate or inanimate. He became 'a living soul.' And the first thing his bleary eyes gazed upon would have been the incomparably beautiful face of his Abba, Father. And the soul that was now alive would have rejoiced.

Take a moment to wonder at the honour God gave to the first man.

The good news is this: men have a special place of honour in heaven because of the way in which God formed and filled the first man.

No wonder King David can take up his lyre, start strumming, and sing, 'What is man that you are mindful of him and the son of man that you visit him?'

So there is good news. Our position as men is one of great dignity and royal nobility in the sight of heaven.

But there is also bad news and the bad news is this — that while positionally we are regarded with extraordinary honour, behaviourally we do not live up to our calling and are capable of deeds of great dishonour.

These deeds began with the Fall of Man when Adam, along with his wife Eve, chose to elevate himself to a status that was not rightfully his. Adam chose to join his wife in eating the forbidden fruit of the knowledge of good and evil — a knowledge which at that time of pristine innocence was the prerogative of God alone. In seeking to ascend to a position of divine privilege, Adam sought to become the Creator rather than the created. He laid himself open to the same charge that God brings to Israel in Isaiah 29.16, 'you are confused. You think the clay is equal to the potter. You think that an object can tell the one who made it, "You didn't make me." This is like a pot telling its maker, "You don't know anything."'

What was lost in this moment of madness?

The first thing that was lost had to do with relating. Up until the Fall of Man, Adam had related to his heavenly Father as a son. The genealogy of Jesus in the first chapter of Luke's Gospel clearly shows this (Luke 3.38). Originally Adam had the status of a son. His heavenly Father created him. He also named him. He called him 'Adam', a deliberate and delightful wordplay on 'adamah', meaning 'dust' or 'clay.' Adam was formed from *adamah*. Dusty was made from the dust.

The first thing that was lost had to do with relating. Adam was created as a son made in the image of God. In other words, he was a son who was created to reflect accurately and clearly what his heavenly Father was like. When Adam fell, his intimacy was destroyed and his identity distorted. No longer was he a son, he was an orphan, separated by sin from Abba's love.

The second thing that was lost had to do with ruling. As we have already seen, God's original mandate to both Adam and Eve was to be fruitful, multiply, replenish, subdue and have dominion. In other words, Adam's mandate was to take the culture of heaven that he enjoyed in the Garden of Eden and, with Eve by his side (and their offspring too), take it to the whole earth.

Now here we have to ask an intriguing question. 'Was the world outside Eden in the same perfect condition as Eden itself?'

To this we believe we need to answer with a 'no.' God's original mandate to Adam and Eve involved filling and subduing the earth and bringing the dominion or the rule of God to the whole of creation.

This suggests that there was something about the landscape outside Eden that was imperfect, unformed, disordered and incomplete. How else can we imagine it? If God tasked Adam to take the rule of God into the world outside Eden, then that world must have needed to be brought into loving alignment with the Father's order. This was accordingly the adventure to which the first man and the first woman (and indeed the sons of Adam and the daughters of Eve) were enlisted; they were called to the adventure of ruling.

What kind of dominion was this meant to be? This ruling was not to take the form of militant oppression. It was meant to take the form of loving service. Adam and Eve were created to bring the Father's reign to the whole world. They were to bring all things into that same shalom that they enjoyed in Eden. They were to bring order to the disordered, completion to the incomplete, and names to the unnamed. But this meant dominion not domination, liberation not oppression.

Put like that, one can quickly see that man's original destiny was exhilarating. It was not a destiny that meant staying in Eden and gardening ad infinitum. That for many men would be a desperate picture! Rather, it was a call to explore, to pioneer, to tame, to advance and to name. It was a calling to a journey of epic exploration. It was a mandate quite literally to change the world.

Two things were therefore lost when Adam fell — first his right to relate; second his right to rule, and both of these things were inextricably connected to Adam being created 'in the image or likeness of God.' In its simplest sense, this meant that Adam was originally formed to resemble God, both through his identity (sons reflect their fathers) and his destiny (sons do what their fathers do).

This in turn meant a radical deterioration in Adam's manhood and his masculinity.

Adam lost his manhood at the Fall because he lost his inner life — his life of intimacy with the Father. In his soul, he went from being a son to an orphan. It is hard to imagine anything more tragic than this.

At the same time Adam lost his masculinity because he became detached from his original, outward purpose. Instead of being a healing warrior sent out to bring the shalom of heaven to earth, he now became a man who endlessly tilled the stubborn soil, wiping the sweat from his furrowed brow. It is hard to imagine a greater demotion than that.

The tragedy of all this is that every man since Adam has had to live with this same marred and scarred image of God within. All men are spiritual orphans, longing for the intimacy of sons. All men find themselves labouring in the fields, when they could be seated on thrones.

As the Apostle Paul put it in Romans 5.12, 'through one man sin entered the world, and death through sin, and thus death spread to all men, because all sinned.'

The virus spread from Eden to all men.

Since Adam, every man has had to live with the faded image of God within.

BEHOLD THE MAN

Chapter 4:

COMETH THE HOUR

From the time of Adam's expulsion from the Garden of Eden, men lived with a faded image of God. They lost their manhood because their inner world was deprived of the intimacy and rest that came from relating as sons to the Father. They also lost their masculinity because their outer world became one of striving to eke out a living rather than one of ruling.

From the first chapters of Genesis onwards, the big story of the Bible confirms this time after time. When God chooses Israel to become his adopted son, Israel rebels against the Father's love, opting for slavery instead of sonship. Given the opportunity to relate to God in a national sense as a son, Israel constantly responds with the heart of an orphan, going their own way rather than God's way.

Anyone who has read the beginning of Hosea 11 will know that this is the recurring tragedy of Israel's Old Testament history. Who could not be moved by these powerful words of lament which pour forth from the broken heart of the Father?

When Israel was a child I loved him,
And out of Egypt I called my son...
I taught Ephraim to walk,
Taking them by their arms
But they did not know that I healed them.

If Israel rejects the offer to relate, it also abdicates its responsibility to rule. Remember the destiny which God promised to Abram?

'In you, all the families of the earth will be blessed' (Genesis 12.3). God's mandate to Israel was not just to receive a blessing; it was to be a blessing and to the whole earth.

What this meant in essence was that Israel was given the possibility of ruling again. It was given the opportunity to take the Father's blessing from its own borders to every nation on the earth, however pagan, however unworthy. As a nationally adopted son, Israel was called to take the rule of a loving Father to the ends of the earth.

But here again Israel failed to fulfil its part of the covenant with God. Instead of taking the Father's love to the Gentile nations, Israel set up walls to separate itself from the great unclean beyond its borders. By the time Jesus started preaching, there was even a wall set up in the Second Temple precincts which prevented non-Jews from entering the area beyond the so-called Court of the Gentiles, and on pain of death.

Israel therefore failed to seize its destiny.

It was for this reason that God took the initiative. At a particular moment in a particular place, God came to earth himself.

Cometh the hour, cometh the man!

Or in this case, cometh the hour, cometh the God-Man!

As the Apostle Paul said, 'when the fullness of the time had come, God sent forth his Son, born of a woman.'

The Son's name was Jesus, or Yeshua to give it its original version. The mother's name was Mary, Miriam in the original language.

What was really going on in the manger in Bethlehem when the Infant Jesus took his first gulp of earth's oxygen? The most important thing of all to remember is this — that in the Christ Child, God became flesh. In the birth of Jesus, the infinite became an infant. The baby boy crying in the manger was the human face of God. He was 'God with skin' — Yahweh in human flesh.

In this respect, Jesus of Nazareth must never be reduced to a mere teacher or prophet, however great. He is God stepping down into the muck and mire of this fallen planet. Jesus is Lord. He is Adonai. He is Elohim. He is Yahweh. He is God.

But he is also a man, and a man born into a particular culture. Jesus of Nazareth was born in a first century Jewish home and circumcised on the eighth day of his life. He grew up and studied the Hebrew Scriptures and learned from his teachers about the Torah. He used Aramaic as his mother tongue and Hebrew when discussing religious matters. He not only studied, he also worked with his hands, helping his father in a small construction business, and inheriting his father's knowledge and skills. He went to the synagogue every Shabbat and visited the Temple in Jerusalem at the time of the three great pilgrim festivals.

Jesus would have become an adult at his Bar Mitzvah and continued studying and building until he was in his late twenties. Aged about thirty, he was baptised in the River Jordan and began his ministry. When he went about teaching the crowds, he used familiar Jewish ways of communicating like the mashal or parable and familiar terms from the Jewish liturgy, like 'the kingdom of God.' He would most likely have had dark eyes and dark hair as well as a workman's hands and a well tanned face. He was a Jewish man and the Jewish Messiah.

Jesus of Nazareth was accordingly fully God, but he was also fully human.

He was from a realm outside time, yet lived as a man of his time.

As the Council of Chalecdon decreed: 'We, then, following the holy Fathers, all with one consent, teach people to confess one and the same Son, our Lord Jesus Christ, the same perfect in Godhead and also perfect in manhood; truly God and truly man.'

There is no man more remarkable than Jesus of Nazareth.

BEHOLD THE MAN

Chapter 5:

THE LAST ADAM

One of the finest hymns in the New Testament is quoted by the Apostle Paul in his letter to the church in Philippi:

Let this mind be in you which was also in Christ Jesus, who, being in the form of God, did not consider it robbery to be equal with God, but made Himself of no reputation, taking the form of a bondservant, and coming in the likeness of men. And being found in appearance as a man, He humbled Himself and became obedient to the point of death, even the death of the cross. Therefore God also has highly exalted Him and given Him the name which is above every name, that at the name of Jesus every knee should bow, of those in heaven, and of those on earth, and of those under the earth, and that every tongue should confess that Jesus Christ is Lord, to the glory of God the Father.

[Philippians 2.5-11]

It is sometimes argued by the sceptics that it was not until the time of the fourth century AD, specifically at the time of the Council of Chalcedon (AD 451), that Jesus was regarded as divine. Many have tried to make this case academically. The novelist Dan Brown gave it a fresh and more popular twist in his controversial best seller, *The Da Vinci Code*.

Passages like the one I've just quoted reveal how foolish this argument is because it shows that Christians in the fifty years after Jesus' death were already honouring Jesus of Nazareth in terms that were reserved for God alone.

As early as AD60, the Christian congregation in Philippi was singing a hymn in praise of Christ's divinity.

There are so many details in this hymn which tell us about the unique qualities of Jesus Christ.

Perhaps the main thing to notice is the way in which this hymn indirectly extols Jesus as the Last Adam. The First Adam had sought to become equal with God and had reached for something that had not belonged to him by right. His sin was the sin of disobedience. His character flaw was pride.

In this hymn, Jesus Christ is depicted as exactly the reverse. The hymn says that Jesus did not seek to cling onto equality with God but was prepared to lay the attributes of divinity aside in the interests of a lost planet. His virtue was the virtue of obedience. His character was one of self-emptying humility.

What an extraordinary contrast!

The First Adam sought upward mobility, reaching for the attributes of divinity in a desperate and disastrous hubris.

The Last Adam sought downward mobility, divesting himself of the attributes of divinity in a history-making act of humility.

Jesus is truly the Last Adam. He is God become man.

Now all of this is strikingly relevant to the issues of manhood and masculinity. The truth is men can choose. They can choose to live with the mindset of the First Adam or they can choose to live with the mindset of the Last Adam. For Paul, the choice is straightforward. At the beginning of the hymn, he tells the Philippian church to have the mindset of Christ Jesus.

What does it mean to have the mindset of the Last Adam? It means being prepared to let go of prestige and power in the interests of others. It means being prepared to engage in servant leadership — the leadership of the water jug and the towel. It means caring more about relationships than reputation. It means self-death rather than self-indulgence. It means a life of humility not pride, obedience not sinfulness. All of these things are true of the man Jesus.

At the end of his first letter to the Corinthians, Paul explores the difference between the First and the Last Adam. In verses 47-49 of chapter 15 he writes this:

The first man was of the earth, made of dust; the second man is the Lord from heaven. As was the man of dust, so also are those who are made of dust; and as is the heavenly Man, so also are those who are heavenly. And as we have borne the image of the man of dust, we shall also bear the image of the heavenly Man.

Here Paul contrasts the man of dust with the man of heaven. The man of dust is clearly the First Adam, who was formed out of *adamah*, dust. The man of heaven is clearly the Last Adam, Jesus Christ, whom Paul calls 'Lord' (a title he reserves for Jesus) and who came from heaven to earth for our sakes.

He then contrasts two types of people. The first are those who have never met the Heavenly Man — that is to say, Jesus Christ. Such people are men of dust and they bear the image of the man of dust, the First Adam. But then there is a second type of person — the one who has met the Heavenly Man and is now living in Christ. That person still bears the image of the man of dust but now also bears the image of the Heavenly Man as well.

For Christian men, there is a choice to be made with regards to manhood and masculinity.

If manhood is a man's inner world, then the choice is to live with a humble, obedient and selfless heart.

If masculinity is a man's outer world, then the choice is to live a life of self-sacrificial love, exhibiting the qualities of the Servant King.

Those who choose the redemptive version of manhood and masculinity carry and exhibit the image of the Heavenly Man.

In short, they conform to the image of Christ — the Last Adam.

BEHOLD THE MAN

Chapter 6:

RELATING AND RULING

The original mandate given to the First Adam was, as we have seen, a mandate to relate and to rule. Adam was called to relate to the Father as a son and he was called to bring the Father's loving reign to the untamed world outside the borders of Eden.

No one should be in any doubt about what was lost to him and to all men at the Fall. When Adam chose to grasp what was not rightfully or legally his, he did not find himself upwardly mobile at all. Quite the opposite! He found himself falling from a place of great prestige and purpose and taking the rest of the human race with him. What a tragedy in the deepest sense of the word. What a flaw and what a fall.

The good news, however, is this: that Jesus Christ is the Last Adam, the Man from Heaven, who has come into this world to reverse the curse of the Fall and to restore the original mandate to every man who would follow him.

So Jesus Christ himself offers us a model of relating — specifically relating as a son to the Father.

Of course, Jesus is no ordinary son. He is the Son by nature while every man who chooses to follow him becomes a son by adoption. We should never forget this. When Jesus was baptised in the River Jordan, the heavens opened and the Father spoke, 'this is my Son!' This was not an adoption into sonship. This was an affirmation of an already existing and indeed eternal sonship.

Jesus is therefore the one who relates to God as Son and who restores to humankind the Edenic right to relate. He calls God Abba and invites all his followers to call God Abba too.

If Jesus Christ offers us a model of relating, he also offers a model of ruling.

Directly after his baptism, Jesus of Nazareth is compelled to go into the wilderness to combat his enemy, ha satan, the adversary of God. We might put it this way: after the revelation in the river comes the devil in the desert. For forty days and nights Jesus resists the enemy's temptations. Unlike the First Adam, the Last Adam does not succumb to the adversary's attempts to seduce him with the intoxicating promise of power. Jesus conquers his enemy and he does so by non-violent resistance not through a militaristic display of celestial weaponry.

From the desert, the Holy Spirit leads Jesus out into Galilee where he announces that the time has been fulfilled and the Kingdom of God is near. In other words, Jesus begins to usher in the reign of God which is the culture of heaven. He demonstrates and inaugurates this heavenly rule by

Healing the sick
Cleansing the lepers
Delivering the demonised
Preaching good news to the poor
Raising the dead
Ministering to the marginalized
Throwing banquets for the broken
And so on.

Jesus took the reign of heaven — the all-inclusive, life-changing power of the Father's love — to the marginalised people whom the rich and religious neglected and despised. He brought heaven to those who were experiencing hell on earth.

After his death, resurrection and ascension, Jesus Christ poured out the Holy Spirit upon all those who put their trust in him.

That same Holy Spirit is available to men today.

A man filled with the Holy Spirit can have the original Adamic mandate restored in his life.

The Holy Spirit is the Spirit of adoption who fills a man's heart with the revelation that he is a son of the most High God. The same Holy Spirit releases the cry 'Abba, Father' from his heart and his lips. As that happens, the man of God begins to enjoy the right to relate which was lost by the First Adam but regained by the Last.

Similarly, the Holy Spirit is the Spirit of empowerment who enables and equips a man for extraordinary acts of service. The Holy Spirit releases the power of God in our lives so that the man of God can do the works of Jesus, including preach good news and heal the sick. In the process he begins to enjoy the right to rule.

It is hard not give Christ praise when we think of these things!

What all this means is that the man who follows Jesus Christ can have both his manhood and his masculinity gloriously restored.

Internally (in the area of his manhood) he has his identity as a son restored. He calls God *Abba, Father* and knows that he is the object of an unrelenting affirmation and affection from his divine Father.

Externally (in the area of his masculinity) he has his *authority* as a ruler restored. He is empowered to extend the rule of heaven not through a strategy of oppressive domination but through an attitude of loving dominion.

When this happens, the old Adamic man dies and the new, Christ-like man is born.

The Christ-like man is a man who relates to God as a son and rules over his sphere of influence as a servant.

The more a man is led and influenced by the Spirit, the more he is conformed to the image of Christ.

All this is made possible because of the man Christ Jesus. Both in the life that he lived and the death that he died he restores the Edenic 'man-date'.

He gives us the chance to be men like him — relating to the Father as royal sons and reigning in our world as servant rulers.

With Christ, the adventure can begin again.

Chapter 7:

GREATER THAN CAESAR

There is no more appropriate way to end this section on 'Biblical Man' than by returning to the great hymn of praise in Philippians 2.5-11 and contrasting the man Jesus Christ with Caesar. Who is the more impressive as an archetype of the manly man — the King of Kings or the Emperor? Which picture best represents an inspiring model of manhood and masculinity — the God who became a man or the man who wanted to become a god?

Before we answer these questions, let's remember the cultural context in which Paul wrote this letter.

It is very important at this point to remember that Philippi was a 'Rome from Rome.' In other words, it was a Roman colony that sought to be as close as possible to the culture of the city of Rome. Philippi was where veterans of the Roman army retired. It was the city where surviving Roman gladiators went to live out their remaining years. It had a Roman amphitheatre, Roman games, occasional visits from the Roman emperor, and a thoroughly Romanised culture.

It is in this city that a hymn is composed about the supremacy of Jesus Christ. This hymn is quoted by Paul in Philippians 2.5-11. What is extraordinary about it is the way in which the original composer of the hymn chose language which was so subversive within his culture. He used devotional language and ideas that would have been associated with the Imperial Cult (the worship of the Emperor) and used them about Jesus. He did this not to suggest that Jesus Christ was a worthy object of devotion alongside Caesar but to highlight that Jesus Christ was the true Lord of the cosmos.

Let's take the opening words.

Let this mind be in you which was also in Christ Jesus, who, being in the form of God, did not consider it robbery to be equal with God, but made Himself of no reputation, taking the form of a bondservant, and coming in the likeness of men.

What is the Phillipian hymn writer saying here? He is saying that Jesus Christ is the exact opposite of Caesar. In the Imperial Cult, Caesar Augustus was a man whom his culture turned into a god. While there is some debate about the degree to which Augustus wanted this attribution, there is no debate about whether some of his successors desired it. The Roman Emperor Vespasian's last words were reported to have been *'vae, puto deus fio'*. 'Woe is me! I think I'm becoming a god.'

Jesus Christ represents the exact opposite of this self-deifying impulse. He was not a man who longed to have the status of divinity. He was the Son of God who willingly laid aside the attributes of divinity to become a man.

What a contrast!

History is filled with men who aspired to become deities. But it tells of only one deity who aspired to become a man — Jesus Christ.

And this is history not mythology.

It is because Jesus Christ emptied himself and became a man, indeed a humble servant, that he represents a very different model of manhood and masculinity from the Imperial ideal of his day.

Jesus Christ allowed himself to be crucified on a Roman Cross after being sentenced to death by a Roman prefect and flogged to the point of death by hardened Roman legionaries.

He did this out of obedience to the perfect will of the Father and out of extreme love for humankind.

Jesus Christ is therefore the only man worthy of the titles given to Caesar — 'Saviour of the World', 'Lord', 'God', 'Son of God', etc.

As the hymn writer of Philippi put it:

Therefore God also has highly exalted Him and given Him the name which is above every name, that at the name of Jesus every knee should bow, of those in heaven, and of those on earth, and of those under the earth, and that every tongue should confess that Jesus Christ is Lord, to the glory of God the Father.

Jesus alone is worthy of the honorific titles that an idolatrous empire was conferring on a mere mortal.

His name alone is worthy of universal adoration — in heaven and earth and indeed under the earth.

Truly Christ is Lord!

And in the very act of saying that, Christian men who seek to follow and imitate their radical Rabbi sign up to a model of manhood and masculinity that is fashioned in the image of Christ not the image of Caesar.

That was dangerous then and it is dangerous now.

But Christian men were never called to be conformed to the images of manly men in their earthly culture. They were always called to be transformed through the renewing of their minds and conformed to the image of the manly man from heaven — Jesus Christ the Lord.

In Part 2, we will see how drastically these two models of manly men differ from one another.

BEHOLD THE MAN

PART 2:

ROMAN MAN

BEHOLD THE MAN

PROLOGUE

Think of the archetypal image of a Roman man and you will probably end up picturing Russell Crowe dressed as General Maximus, sitting astride his stallion, preparing to lead a cavalry charge, and shouting, 'What we do in life echoes in eternity!' And all this to the accompaniment of Hans Zimmer's rousing and booming soundtrack.

I am referring here, of course, to Sir Ridley Scott's blockbuster movie, *Gladiator*, a film about a Roman General whose family is killed by the Emperor Commodus. The story arc of this film charts Maximus' escape from Commodus' assassins and his life as a gladiator, leading eventually to his involvement in the Games in Rome and a final confrontation with the Emperor.

Part of the reason *Gladiator* is so compelling is because it tells a story about a man who is the epitome of what a Roman male was called to be. Maximus, after all, is strong, self-controlled, prudent, merciful, honourable, courageous, loyal, impressive, just — everything, in fact, that was expected of 'the manly man.' In Western cultures, this is still an arresting and appealing image of masculinity.

Gladiator is also compelling because the Emperor Commodus (acted by Joachim Phoenix) represents everything that the Emperor of Rome was supposed not to be. The Emperor was expected to be an inspiring image of manhood and masculinity. But Commodus is not that at all — he is weak, out of control, unwise, merciless, shameful, disloyal, unimpressive and unjust.

All this talk of *Gladiator* is just our way of introducing you to the idea of the manly man in the Roman Empire of Jesus' day. That is the theme of Part 2 of this book. If in Part 1 we looked at and described Biblical Man (with Jesus, the Last Adam, as the image of that), now in Part 2 we turn to look at Roman Man (with Caesar Augustus as the primary image).

Before we begin, however, one thing needs to be acknowledged and that is the challenge of defining what the Romans understood by 'the manly man.' The difficulty stems from the fact that the critical concept which defined Roman masculinity, *virtus*, is itself a slippery one. It is actually no simple matter to find out what qualities were implied by this term.

One problem with *virtus* is that it changed its meaning over time. During the early, middle and late eras of Roman history, the word shifted from denoting a range of martial qualities (such as courage in battle) to a word that also denoted a range of more ethical qualities (like justice and fairness). It shifted from referring to a good soldier to referring to a good man, especially in the political sphere.

Another problem with *virtus* consists of the fact that at no point was it ever agreed what qualities were implied by the word. There are four things that are regarded as almost canonical or cardinal qualities — fortitude, prudence, temperance and justice — but these 'manly' qualities are not always mentioned in ancient discussions of virtus and often new qualities are added.

All this is to say that *virtus* is something of a moving target. It is hard to lock on to a single meaning and a settled list of all the manly qualities expected.

Having said all that there is a very helpful quotation in an ancient text by Xenophon of Athens, who lived four hundred years before Jesus, which helps us in our quest.

Xenophon was a philosopher, historian and soldier, as well as a contemporary of Socrates (whom he greatly admired).

In his work entitled *Cyropaedia* (about the education of King Cyrus the Great), Xenophon wrote about the ideal ruler. He used Cyrus as a model. This is what he wrote:

'The good king must be a model to his subjects; by his virtues he ensures the continued well-being of his commonwealth. Hence, through his actions he shows himself possessed of the noblest virtues: piety towards gods and men, wisdom, courage and prowess in battle, temperance, generosity, faithfulness and love of truth.'

Here Xenophon lists seven things that he saw in Cyrus:

- Piety
- Wisdom
- Courage
- Temperance
- Generosity
- Faithfulness
- Love of truth

Notice that he calls them 'virtues'.

It is now agreed that these seven qualities entered the Roman world as well and inspired the cult of virtues perpetuated by the Roman Emperors.

Furthermore, these seven qualities became essential ingredients not only of the Emperor's leadership but also of his masculinity. The Emperor was expected to be like Cyrus, if you will — a man who was pious, wise, courageous, temperate, generous, faithful, and truth-loving. The first Emperor of Rome — Caesar Augustus — embodied all of these and more.

What we propose to do in the second part of this book is to define these seven virtues, look at how they appeared in the life of Augustus and his devotees, compare and contrast how they feature in the life of Christ and his disciples, before finally asking, 'who's the real man?'

Or, to use the Roman terminology, 'who's the manly man?'

BEHOLD THE MAN

Chapter 1:

PIETY

In Roman society you were born male *(homo)* but you made yourself a man *(vir)*. To do that, you had to cultivate certain virtues in your life, one of which was *pietas*, translated as 'religious devotion.' *Pietas* referred to reverential attention to the gods of Ancient Rome.

Many Roman citizens in the time of Christ still believed in a reality beyond the natural and the physical world and they believed that this spiritual dimension, inhabited by the gods, affected and influenced their material world.

As with all the manly virtues, the Emperor was expected to be a supreme and inspiring example of pietas. In other words, he was expected to embody and exhibit reverential attention to the gods more than any other man.

In this the Emperor Augustus did not disappoint. Even his name points to his religious devotion. 'Augustus' means literally 'the revered one' and was conferred on him because he was regarded as holy and venerable.

Early on in his career Augustus had sought to prove his manly virtue through martial prowess — through displays of military bravery and excellence, as at his famous victory at the Battle of Actium.

Later on in his life, Augustus turned to more spiritual proofs of his manliness, assuming a priestly role and even earning the title,

Pontifex Maximus (chief priest of the civic institutions).

Part of the reason for this religious veneration of the Emperor Augustus was his liturgical and leading involvement in the priestly colleges of Rome, some of which he himself revived. But the primary reason for this devotion centred on his extensive building programme in Rome and its environs, much of which involved the building and rebuilding of religious temples at his own expense.

In his own account of his achievements — the *Res Gestae Divi Augusti* ('The Deeds Done by the Divine Augustus', written in AD 14, just before his death) — Augustus summarises some of his contributions in this area:

'I built ... the temple of Apollo on the Palatine with the porticos, the temple of divine Julius ... the temple on the Capitoline of Jupiter Subduer and Jupiter Thunderer, the temple of Quirinius, the temple of Lares at the top of holy street, the temple of the gods of the Penates on the Velian, the temple of Youth, and the temple of the Great Mother on the Palatine. I rebuilt eighty two temples of the gods in the city by the authority of the senate, omitting nothing which ought to have been rebuilt at that time.'

From this evidence there can be no questioning Augustus' pietas. He was a man's man — exhibiting a spiritual and religious commitment that pointed to his noble honouring of the gods of Ancient Rome.

What is further interesting about Augustus' piety is the way in which his position as Emperor and his performance as Pontifex Maximus led to him being venerated as more than human — in short as divine.

It isn't long before Augustus is being referred to as *divus filius*, a 'son of god.' His piety — expressed through his priestly conduct — earned him divine titles and the expectation of a place among the gods at his death.

Mention of the title 'son of god', of course, brings us to Augustus' contemporary, Jesus of Nazareth. When we compare the piety of Caesar with the piety of Christ, the differences could not be more marked. Jesus of Nazareth exhibited pietas, but his piety was not grounded in a belief in the gods of Rome but in God the Father, and his position as 'Son of God' was not earned through pious performance but was an eternal, unchanging reality.

Let's briefly expand on these two points.

First of all, Jesus did not worship the ancient gods of Rome. He worshipped one whom he called Abba. Indeed, the prayer he taught his disciples begins with the words, 'Our Father.'

An accurate English translation of this word is hard to establish. The word Abba was in use in Jesus' day in Jewish family settings (and still is today), where children referred to their father as abba and their mother as *imma*. Abba means something like 'daddy', 'papa', or 'dearest father.' *Imma* means 'mummy', 'mama' or 'dearest mother.' Both words denote familiarity and respect, intimacy and honour.

When Jesus used the word *Abba* in his teaching about God, and indeed in his prayers to God, he was breaking theological ground. While there is meagre evidence that other Jewish sages at the time referred to God as 'father' (which we should expect, given the Old Testament uses of this name for God), the use of *Abba* in Jesus' worship and instruction was something distinctive. It pointed not only to his unusually intimate relationship with God (as his Papa) but also to his deep sense of his own Sonship — of his status as Son.

We must therefore understand that Jesus the man was not like Augustus at all. He did not worship pagan deities. He worshipped and adored the One who created the Universe and whom he called his 'Dearest Father.'

More than that, Jesus did not earn the right to be called 'Son of God' on the basis of his *res gestae* or good works (as Caesar Augustus had). He was already God's Son before he had done anything!

All this is resoundingly confirmed at his baptism in the River Jordan. As Jesus comes out of the water, the heavens are torn open and the Father declares, 'this is my Beloved Son in whom I am well pleased.'

Note two things here.

First, as we stressed earlier in this book, this declaration of Jesus' position is not an adoption but an affirmation. In other words, Jesus does not *become* God's Son at his baptism. He is affirmed as already *being* Son.

Jesus has always been, and will forever be, God's only Son *by nature.*

The second thing we should notice is that the Father's affirmation of Jesus' Sonship is not based on Jesus' *res gestae* because Jesus has not begun his public ministry yet. That will happen after his baptism.

In other words, Jesus' Sonship is not based on his preaching the Good News of the Kingdom, healing the sick, delivering the demonised, cleansing the lepers, raising the dead and so on — because he hadn't done any of those things at this stage. It is not, in other words, based on performance.

In light of this, we begin to see the huge gulf between the manly piety of Christ and the manly piety of Caesar.

Caesar's piety was focused upon pagan gods. Christ's on his heavenly Father.

Caesar's piety was based on his performance. Christ's was based on his position.

The Emperors of Rome came to be known as *divus* and as *divus filius.* But the One who truly deserves such titles is not the Emperor of Rome but the Carpenter from Nazareth.

Jesus' entire life was accordingly one of a new, radical and subversive piety.

He exhibited a very different manliness from Caesar. Caesar's piety was an external reality, demonstrated by outward actions. Jesus' piety was an internal reality, demonstrated by a unique and history making intimacy with his Father.

In light of all this we should ask, what are the implications for Christian men?

The answer is this — Christian men are to embrace a piety of internal, personal relationship with the Father and this is to be the foundational reality of their lives. It is to be the warp core of their manhood and masculinity.

How does a man in today's world enter in to such a position as a son?

In his two letters to church congregations planted in Roman provinces, the Apostle Paul talks about this when he talks about spiritual adoption.

In Romans 8.15 he writes:

You did not receive the spirit of bondage again to fear, but you received the Spirit of adoption by whom we cry out 'Abba, Father.'

In Galatians 4.5-6, Paul writes in a similar vein:

When the fullness of the time had come, God sent forth His Son, born of a woman, under the law, to redeem those who were under the law, that we might receive the adoption as sons. And because you are sons, God has sent forth the Spirit of His Son into your hearts, crying out 'Abba, Father!'

I have already indicated that in both cases, Paul is writing to a church based in a Roman province.

It should therefore come as no surprise that Paul chooses to use a word picture from the Roman context when he starts speaking of our salvation in Christ. This word picture is 'adoption.'

Interestingly, there was no rite or process of adoption in the Jewish culture at the time, nor was there any teaching in the Old Testament about how to adopt children (although there are constant references to orphans from Exodus onwards).

Paul was using a Roman not a Jewish metaphor when he addressed these churches.

How then did Romans adopt children? The process involved two steps.

The first consisted of a sale and was known as *mancipatio*.

Usually, a couple who couldn't have children decided to adopt the son of a slave in their own extended household.

The biological father sold his son to the adopting father in a symbolic ritual involving coins and copper scales. He sold him three times to the adopting father and after the third sale the slave's son was handed over for adoption.

The second stage consisted of a formal presentation of the case for adoption by the new father. This took place before a Roman praetor or magistrate and was known in Latin as *vindicatio*.

If the magistrate accepted the case, then he declared the slave's son *sui heredes* — in other words, he declared the slave's son to be the son of his adopting father and the actual heir of everything in the new father's estate.

In the process, the boy was transferred from the *patria potestas* (i.e. the fatherly authority) of his natural father and placed under the patria potestas of his new, adopting father.

This then was a great and undeserved privilege. Through no merit of his own, the son of the slave now found himself enjoying a new father, a new family, a new fortune and, above all, a new freedom.

Now look what happens to this image in the quite breathtakingly brilliant mind of the Apostle Paul, himself a Roman citizen.

In his understanding, we are all of us slaves and the sons of a slave (Satan).

But Christ has come into the world to redeem us — to buy us out of slavery.

Our freedom is purchased not through gold or silver but through the blood of Christ — and through believing in the glorious, finished work of the Cross.

When we do this, we are no longer under the fatherly authority of the father of lies. We are under the fatherly authority of the Father of Lights.

All our previous debts have been cancelled.

Our chains have been irrevocably broken.

Through no merit of our own, we now enjoy a new Father, a new family (the church), a new fortune (our inheritance as co-heirs with Christ) and a new freedom ('the glorious liberty of the children of God').

Christian men accordingly need to grasp this image of adoption.

Christian men need to receive the Spirit of adoption and celebrate the fact that they are sons.

They need to allow the Spirit of adoption to permeate their inner being so that their hearts cry 'Abba, Father' in adoration of the living God.

Christian men are accordingly sons of God.

This is our status. And this is given not earned, internal not external, genuine not counterfeit.

It is a position given to us by grace.

BEHOLD THE MAN

Chapter 2:

WISDOM

The second manly virtue revered by Roman society was known in Latin as *prudentia.* **The translation of this word as 'wisdom' (or 'prudence') is too general. In reality the word had quite a specific connotation.**

Prudentia can be defined as 'proactive reasoning which leads to practical action'. The key here is 'proactive reasoning.' The word *prudentia* is itself a clue to this because it is a contraction of the word *providentia,* meaning foresight.

In warfare, a General anticipates the moves that his enemy will make and exhibits *prudentia* in his proactive decisions — either secretly positioning men to thwart an advance or conducting a surprise attack before his enemy does.

In the political arena, the politician anticipates the moves that his opponents will make and demonstrates *prudentia* by making proactive decisions — ones which defuse the power of his enemies' plans and arguments.

In both contexts, then, whether military or political, *prudentia* refers to a level of strategic and discerning thinking which is way above the ordinary — one which earns a leader the right to be known as full of *virtu* or manly strength.

This brings us once again to the greatest of all the Roman leaders, the Emperor Augustus. If ever there was a man in the Roman political and public sphere that embodied *prudentia* it is

Caesar Augustus.

That Caesar Augustus was a wise and successful statesman as well as an extremely shrewd politician is evidenced by the fact that he reigned for nearly 45 years as Emperor and inaugurated two hundred years of peace in the Roman Empire.

Space does not permit a full account of how Augustus showed *prudentia* so one example among countless will have to suffice — and this concerns his response to the four main challenges he faced as he took power: 1) the threat of the Germans in the northern borders of the Empire; 2) the size of the army, which was so large it had created a state within a state; 3) the poverty of the urban population and the rural farmers; 4) the loss of confidence and power in the Senate.

Augustus responded to all these challenges in his reforms in the 20s BC. He first of all made the decision that the Empire was not to extend any further north but consolidate its existing territories south of the Rhine and Danube Rivers — thereby strengthening a frontier that had become alarmingly weak. To do this he created four new provinces — Rhaetia, Noricum, Pannonia and Moesia — which he designated Imperial Provinces, governed by *legati* who were accountable to him alone and forbidden by him to oppress their subjects.

He secondly reduced the size of the Roman army from 60 to 28 legions (a maximum of 150,000 men) and gave a cash settlement to all soldiers who had served over 20 years (thereby ensuring their allegiance to him not their Generals). He also removed all Roman soldiers from the city of Rome (where they had had a nasty habit of meddling in civic affairs) and established the 9000 strong Praetorian Guard, to protect him and to keep order in the city.

Thirdly, Augustus improved conditions in Rome by establishing a city police force under a *praefectus urbi,* a fire and detective department under a *praefectus vigilum,* and a proper grain distribution system under a *praefectus annonae.* He started to build a permanent civil service from Rome, through Italy to the Provinces, creating a robust administrative system which meant that workers

— especially farmers — were not exploited by tax collectors.

Fourthly, he reduced the size of the Senate from 1000 to 800 by excluding the 'provincials' and freedmen that Julius Caesar had admitted and he restored the Senate's dignity by making it an advisory body in his decision making. In doing this, he restored some of the kudos that the Senate had enjoyed in previous times while at the same time ensuring that these powers of legislation were restricted to serving his leadership.

Augustus was accordingly a master of *prudentia*. However much his wisdom came from the advice of trusted others — especially Agrippa and Maecenas — proactive and strategic decision-making was at the very heart of his leadership.

How then does this compare with the man, Jesus of Nazareth? It should be noted from the start that the Jewish people knew that their coming Messiah would be filled with a spiritual wisdom that was utterly different from anything the world had ever seen. As it says in Isaiah 11.2:

> *The Spirit of the LORD shall rest upon Him*
> *The Spirit of wisdom and understanding*
> *The Spirit of counsel and might*
> *The Spirit of knowledge and the fear of the LORD*

Notice the number of qualities associated with the future Messiah. There will be seven in all (seven being the perfect number in Judaism) — three pairs and one stand-alone quality which precedes them all, the Spirit of the LORD.

This is somewhat reminiscent of the menorah or seven branched candlestick which stood in the Tabernacle of old and then subsequently in the Temple of Solomon and the Second Temple of Zerubbabel.

The *menorah* had one central branch and then three branches either side.

The Messiah to come would have the Spirit of the LORD upon him (the central branch) and then three pairs of qualities deriving from that anointing — wisdom and understanding, counsel and might, knowledge and the fear of the LORD.

The menorah had one central branch and then three branches either side.

Right at the heart of these qualities is wisdom, which in turn is closely allied with understanding, counsel and knowledge. The Coming Messiah would be a man of exceptional, heavenly insight and foresight.

When Jesus appears on the stage of history, his wisdom is regarded as remarkable even from a very early age. In fact, at the age of twelve (i.e. just before becoming a man), he is already astonishing Jerusalem's sages with his wisdom.

When Jesus is baptized in the Holy Spirit in the River Jordan, he begins his public ministry — a ministry in which he shows other-worldly levels of wisdom, understanding, counsel and knowledge.

To cite one among many famous examples, John 8.1-11 describes an incident in which Jesus is confronted by some men, old and young, who have caught a woman in the very act of adultery.

These men — John tells us they were Scribes and Pharisees — bring her dishevelled and ashamed before Jesus and ask him what they should do, given that the Torah teaches that such a person should be stoned to death.

John, as he tells this story, points out that these men were not really interested in catching the woman at all; they were more interested in catching the man in front of them. In short, they were testing Jesus.

What is Jesus to do? If he says, 'stone her to death,' they will accuse him of lacking compassion. If he says, 'let her go,' they will accuse him of lacking obedience. Either way they can accuse him of lacking qualities expected of the Messiah.

It is interesting at this point to notice what John tells us about Jesus' response to the men. He simply tells us that Jesus stooped and started drawing something in the sand with his finger, as if he had not even heard them.

There has been much debate about what Jesus was doing here but the answer is contained within the distinctive word John uses for Jesus' writing here — it is the Greek verb *katagraphein*.

The normal Greek verb that we would expect in this situation is *graphein*, but John uses a technical word from the world of the law courts, a word associated with the writing down of charges brought against an accused person.

In other words, John portrays Jesus writing down in the sand all the charges that God can bring against each of the men — the religious men standing before him — who have so shamed the woman.

When he is done writing down some of these charges — 'adultery', 'fraud', 'dishonesty', 'lying', 'cheating', 'greed', and so on — John tells us that Jesus stands to his full height and addresses them.

'He who is without sin among you, let him throw a stone at her first.'

Actually, this is not the best translation of the word 'sin' here. It really should read, 'He who is without a sinful thought in his head, let him throw a stone at her first.' That's stronger, more intensive, than 'sin.'

Then he goes back to writing some more charges in the sand!

It is fascinating to read what happens next: John tells us that the consciences of all the men were pricked and that they all began to leave, beginning with the older men first (they were old enough to know Jesus had nailed them!).

What a story! What a man!

The wisdom of the man Jesus is extraordinary. It is more than just a rational consideration of all possibilities, with a mixture of strategic insight and foresight, leading to practical action. In short, it is more than man-made *prudentia*.

It is not the wisdom of the natural mind — however brilliant. It is the insight given by the Holy Spirit — the Holy Spirit that rests upon Messiah Jesus, illuminating him with wisdom, understanding, counsel and knowledge (Isaiah 11.2).

No wonder the Apostle Paul describes Jesus Christ as 'the Wisdom of God.' Caesar may exhibit wisdom but Christ embodies wisdom. And his wisdom is greater than the finest wisdom of the ancients.

What, then, are the implications for Christian men today?

While we wouldn't want for a moment to devalue or neglect the use of *prudentia* in military, governmental or indeed any other context, the fact is there is something very different about the wisdom of Jesus. While *prudentia* is the product of the natural, rational mind — the capacity to analyze, synthesize and strategize — the wisdom Jesus exhibits is emphatically supernatural and heavenly in character.

That is not to say that supernatural, heavenly wisdom is somehow non-rational or even irrational. Far from it in fact! We believe that the wisdom given by the Holy Spirit is the most reasonable of all.

So for Christian men, who are seeking to conform to the image of Christ not Caesar, the key implication is simply this: that we continually ask for more of the endowment of wisdom in our public and private life.

The good news is that the Bible encourages us to ask for such wisdom.

If any of you lacks wisdom, let him ask God, who gives to all liberally and without reproach, and it will be given to him.

[James 1.5]

Here there is a promise for all Christian men to grasp and use. If we ask for supernatural wisdom, God — who is the true source of that wisdom and indeed all true wisdom — will grant it.

This wisdom, in turn, is completely effective in its application.

The wisdom that is from above is first of all pure, then peaceable, gentle, willing to yield, without partiality and without hypocrisy.

[James 3.17]

The wisdom that is given by the Holy Spirit brings peace to troubled, chaotic and confusing situations.

Let's take a vivid example. During the Falklands War, Chris Keeble was second in command of the British elite parachute regiment. A devout Christian, Chris — a father of four — had prayed that his experiences would increase his faith.

'I went up to the hills surrounding my home, knelt down in the grass and committed myself to this endeavor in the hope that this experience would be essentially a spiritual one. I did not see it as a military experience at all.' 'I had a great sense of the Holy Spirit,' he added.

It wasn't long before his faith was put to the test. Chris was left in charge of his troops when his commanding officer, Colonel H Jones VC, was killed during a courageous attack on Argentine forces at Goose Green. Chris found himself and his troops outnumbered three to one. It was an utterly hopeless situation and Chris had no desire for any further loss of life. Both sides had suffered heavy casualties and were now engaged in brutal, hand to hand fighting.

For many years, Chris had cherished a very special prayer by a French Trappist monk who had experienced a dramatic conversion while he had been a soldier. Chris had this prayer laminated and he kept it with him at all times. The prayer, by Charles de Foucauld, reads thus:

'Father, I abandon myself into your hands; do with me what you will. Whatever you do I thank you. I am ready for all. I accept all. Let only your will be done in me. I wish for no more than this.'

In the midst of a war-torn situation in which men were being killed, Chris knelt down in the gorse of Goose Green and prayed that prayer, knowing that he only had God to turn to.

What happened next was remarkable. Suddenly Chris knew what he had to do. He took two Argentine POWs and ordered them to go to their CO and tell him that the British were inviting him to surrender in return for the rest of the POWs.

That, Chris later reflected, was totally counter-cultural for his paratroopers. Their culture dictated that they should fight to the death. But this was a peaceful, negotiated alternative to a bloodbath.

The Argentine CO duly surrendered, even though his forces greatly outnumbered Chris' remaining troops, and the battle was ended without further bloodshed — all because of a prayer prayed in desperation.

What a graphic picture of the wisdom that is above — the heavenly wisdom that is gentle and conciliatory, not violent and divisive.

The Roman man may have revered the cultivated virtue of *prudentia*, but the Christian man cultivates the supernatural wisdom that brings peace.

The Christian man accesses a divine wisdom and, by faith and prayer, brings that wisdom from heaven to earth with extraordinary results.

The manly man is a man of heavenly more than earthly prudence.

Chapter 3:

COURAGE

The third great virtue of the Roman man was known as *fortitude,* **translated as courage or bravery. Since virtu meant literally 'acting like a man', fortitude was regarded as an essential quality.**

In Roman society, virtu was seen primarily in outstanding deeds *(egregia facinora).* These great deeds — which mostly consisted of brave actions in military contexts — brought a person honour *(gloria).*

Gloria really meant 'a good reputation' and was regarded as essential for the manly man. First because his *fama* (what people thought of him) was enhanced; secondly, because his *dignitas* (his standing in the community) was increased.

Fama and *dignitas* were essential if a man was to aspire to and achieve public office *(honos).* It was the responsibility of every man in the elite classes of Rome to increase the *dignitas* of his family and one of the primary ways in which he could do that was through exhibiting *fortitude* — bravery in battle.

One famous story of courage in battle, much loved by the Romans, concerned a Roman soldier called Horatius Cocles, who held a bridge against an advancing Etruscan army led by Lars Porsenna in the year 510 BC.

Horatius was a Roman officer during the time of the ancient Roman Republic. He found himself with his fellow legionaries at the *Pons Sublicius*, a bridge which *Porsenna* planned to take so that he could enter and sack Rome.

As the enemy began to cross and his own troops started to run in panic, Horatius — who had already lost an eye in an earlier battle (hence his name, *Cocles*, 'one eyed') — grabbed hold of two more senior officers and told them to stand with him. He had to shame the two Generals — named by Livy (*History of Rome* 2.10) as Spurius Lartius and Titus Herminius — into standing with him. Horatius stood his ground, in spite of the fact that he was wounded all over his body, until he heard the shout from his own soldiers that the bridge was now torn up and the enemy could not therefore use it to cross into Rome. Horatius duly threw himself into the river, with his armour still on and his weapons in his hands. In spite of the fact that he had a spear in his buttocks, he managed to swim to his cheering comrades without losing any of his equipment.

Horatius' actions — although partly inspired by legend rather than fact — meant that Porsenna could not sack Rome but had to engage in a long and drawn out siege, which ended in a peace treaty and the city remaining intact.

Horatius was given as much land as he could plough in a single day with a yoke of oxen. A bronze statue of him was erected in the *comitium* (part of the forum). Later Lord Macaulay (1800-1859) immortalised him in the famous lines:

Then out spake brave Horatius,
The Captain of the Gate:
"To every man upon this earth
Death cometh soon or late.
And how can man die better
Than facing fearful odds,
For the ashes of his fathers,
And the temples of his Gods"

The story (taken here from Macaulay's *The Lays of Ancient Rome*) concludes with this rousing finale:

With weeping and with laughter
Still is the story told,

How well Horatius kept the bridge
In the brave days of old.
So much for one-eyed Horatius!

What then of the Emperor Augustus?

There can be no doubt that Caesar Augustus showed *fortitudo* in his former, military campaigns (while he was known as Octavian), and then in his subsequent political leadership of Rome and its Empire.

As we have already seen, Augustus was not shy or retiring about his achievements. Shortly before his death he wrote his own eulogy, known as 'The Deeds Done by the Divine Augustus' (commonly referred to as the *Res Gestae*).

In writing the *Res Gestae*, Augustus included his earlier, military achievements, particularly in his war against Antony and Cleopatra, which culminated in the death of both his enemies and the capture of Egypt and its vast treasure.

Here are a few excerpts from the *Res Gestae*:

'In my nineteenth year, on my own initiative and at my own expense, I raised an army with which I set free the state, which was oppressed by the domination of a faction ...

I drove the men who slaughtered my father into exile with a legal order, punishing their crime, and afterwards, when they waged war on the state, I conquered them in two battles.

I captured six hundred ships in addition to those smaller than triremes.

Twice I triumphed with an ovation, and three times I enjoyed a *curale* triumph. Twenty one times I was named emperor.

In my triumphs, kings and nine children of kings were led before my chariot.'

This is precisely the kind of courage associated with the Roman manly man. Augustus represented the apex of manly *fortitude* in the empire he ruled from 30BC to AD14. Every Roman male aspired to be like him.

What then of the man Jesus? In what sense can he be said to have exhibited *fortitudo*?

The important thing to say here is that Jesus embodied a new courage, not within the realm of bravery on the fields of battle, but a courage which contradicted the philosophies and ideologies within the Jewish nation and Greco-Roman world.

We have already looked at the Roman world, so let's take a quick look at the Jewish world so that we can see just how Jesus subverted Jewish expectations of courage as well.

In the Old Testament, the manly man is often seen — as in the Roman culture — as a person of martial prowess and military courage.

Joshua, the successor to Moses, was commanded by God three times to be 'strong and of good courage…and be very courageous' (Joshua 1.6-9). The Hebrew word *hamats* means 'strong, alert, courageous, brave, stout, bold, swift footed.'

King David was a renowned, skilful soldier of war and his mighty men were feared among the nations (1 Samuel 22.1; 1 Chronicles 11).

God himself is often depicted in the Old Testament as the Divine Warrior, as one who fights for Israel and enables them to prevail against his enemies.

With Jesus, this military picture of courage is totally subverted. Indeed, Jesus exhibits and exemplifies a totally different image to the Hebraic or Hellenistic versions of the 'man of war.' For Jesus, the art of war consists of counter-cultural expressions of courage:

Blessed are the meek, for they shall inherit the earth…blessed are the merciful, for they shall obtain mercy…blessed are the peacemakers, for they shall be called sons of God.

[Matthew 5.3-10]

This shows a very different kind of *fortitudo* and a very different image of manliness and masculinity.

Jesus repeatedly engaged in conflict as he debated the opinions and views of his contemporaries concerning the interpretation and application of the Torah, in which the Pharisees rested their righteousness and hope.

This often led to the questioning of Jesus' own source of power and authority but at no stage did he resort to military means to achieve his God-given mission. At no point did he use either earthly or heavenly weapons to win his conflicts.

Jerome H. Neyrey writes concerning men of this era (and indeed our own), 'it was exclusive male behaviour to seek honour, make claims, and to defend them. It is uniquely male behaviour to engage in combat.' But Jesus nowhere engages in combat. He could have called for twelve legions of angels to deliver him from those who came to arrest him (Matthew 26.53) but he never called upon the armies of heaven. Indeed Jesus rebuked Peter for producing a secreted dagger and cutting off the earlobe of the High Priest's servant, saying 'those who take the sword will perish by the sword.'

Peter and the disciples may have imagined a deliverer much like the warrior-kings in their hyper-masculine world — one who would use violence to establish a new earthly kingdom. But Jesus' actions signalled a new way in which courage was to be understood. Jesus embodied a new 'ideal behaviour' for the manly man — one that bypassed martial prowess expressed through force and aggression.

The Apostle Peter was later to understand this alternative understanding of fortitude very powerfully, as can be seen in the words that he himself penned about his Master and Messiah (1 Peter 2.22-23):

He committed no sin, nor was deceit found in His mouth, who, when He was reviled, did not revile in return; when He suffered, He did not threaten, but committed Himself to Him who judges righteously.

Peter came to understand that Jesus was never meant to come as a Messianic warrior-king, followed by a mighty army, using the military resources of heaven and earth to liberate the land from Roman occupation and oppression. Rather, he saw that Jesus took the full force of Roman punitive law, administered in the cruellest way by members of the Roman army, when he exposed his body to the barbaric torture of his trial, flogging and crucifixion.

This, then, is a very different kind of fortitude. It is not a courage expressed in military aggression. It is a courage expressed through passive, non-violent resistance. This is not victory through victimizing others but victory through becoming a willing victim. This is not a worldly kind of heroism but an altogether heavenly one.

In this Christ showed manhood, expressed in his courageous ability to suffer on behalf of others. According to Christ, it is this attitude of self-sacrificial service that leads to greatness in his Kingdom. With such courage Jesus was able to demonstrate the greatest example of manhood — an innocent man overcoming sin through a vicarious and violent death. Jesus' death is a noble, heroic, manly act. He dies well and he dies for others. He doesn't die for the cause of an Empire but for the cause of the Kingdom.

In this respect, Christ's *fortitudo* is nothing less than a 'new normal' for men. In Christ we see a new kind of virtu — a new image of the manly man. We see a new narrative in which the world is transformed through love not power — a narrative in which men eschew violent means and instead choose the path of non-violent, self-sacrificial service. Such a narrative redefines heroism and merits the word 'epic.'

How are Christian men to respond to this new imagination, this bold, subversive and heroic narrative of manly fortitude?

The answer is clear, though it is not easy. As Christian men, we give our lives as adopted sons in the service of our loving heavenly Father.

In the conflicts that may arise as a result of this primary allegiance to Christ rather than Caesar, we don't respond with macho aggression and military might. We respond with the self-sacrificial and non-violent love of the God revealed by Jesus of Nazareth. In this we show ourselves conformed to the image of Christ rather than the image of Caesar.

The true manly man suffers violence in the faith and hope that this brave absorption of fallen aggression will result long term in the transformation of society. The true man works for change through the power of love (Kingdom), not through the love of power (Empire). In this respect we are called to deny ourselves and take up our cross daily — an action which can sometimes demand the ultimate sacrifice.

Perhaps a story is needed at this point.

In the winter of 320 AD, Licinius, Emperor of the Eastern part of the Roman Empire, broke his agreement with Constantine (Emperor of the West), formulated in the Edict of Milan. In this Lucinius had agreed to end his persecution of Christians.

Lucinius ordered all Roman soldiers to renounce Christianity and to offer a sacrifice to the Roman gods. His edict reached the Thundering Legion at Sabaste and the order was duly passed down to the legionaries.

Forty Christians in the legion withstood threats, beatings, and torture and refused to obey the edict, choosing instead to obey a higher authority. They declared, 'You shall have no other gods before me. You shall not make for yourself an idol, whether in the form of anything that is in heaven above, or that is on the earth beneath, or that is in the water under the earth. You shall not bow down to them or worship them.'

In retaliation, the legion marched the men to a frozen lake where they were ordered to remove their armour and clothing and stand naked, as a form of slow execution, on a frozen lake.

The legionaries lit a large fire on the shore with a warm bath and food to tempt the Christians to make the pagan sacrifice, renounce their Christian faith, and save their lives. The commander told them, 'You may come ashore when you are ready to deny your faith.' But the men began to pray, 'O Lord, forty wrestlers have come forth to fight for Thee. Grant that forty wrestlers may gain the victory!'

The mother of the youngest legionary was present. She called out to him from the shore, where the warm fire and hot bath was beckoning, and enticed her son to abandon the others. However, there was a centurion on the bank called Sempronius. He watched as the remaining Christian legionaries continued to cry out, 'O Lord, forty wrestlers have come forth to fight for thee. Grant that forty wrestlers may gain the victory!' In response to this extraordinary bravery, Centurion Sempronius confessed Jesus as Christ, removed his armour, weapons and clothing, walked across the ice and joined the thirty nine Christian soldiers on the lake. The next morning the forty martyrs of Sabaste (as they came to be known) were found dead on the ice. Their faithful resistance has been recorded for all time in the annals of history.

This is true courage. This is Christian *fortitudo*.

This is the conduct of the manly man in the Kingdom of God!

Caesar Augustus ruled through the use of force. As one historian, H.H. Scullard, puts it, 'the ultimate sanction of his authority was force, however much it was disguised.'

Christ Jesus rules the world through the use of non-violent heroism.

And Christian men are called to follow suit.

Chapter 4:

TEMPERANCE

One of the greatest virtues that a Roman man was encouraged to embrace was known as *temperantia*, the ability to master oneself, especially under pressure. For Roman men, this virtue was essential in all kinds of leadership, not just military leadership. The Roman man had to be able to master and control his own nature if he was to be a leader of other men. For the Roman man, it was impossible to think of managing other people if you couldn't first manage yourself. No Roman man could really be said to have virtu if he didn't possess *temperantia*. If a Roman man didn't possess *temperantia*, it revealed that he was fit to be ruled but not to rule.

What set the *vir* (the manly man) apart from a mere homo (a man) was the ability to control himself through discipline and willpower. This was because the Roman man knew that there was no way he could ever lead others if he couldn't first lead himself. If leadership is about influence, then the Roman man understood that he needed to exercise a restraining influence over himself before he could have any credibility or ability in doing so with others, especially in public life.

Temperantia is accordingly a vital aspect of Roman *virtu*. At the heart of *temperantia* is the idea of control over excess. Therefore, a number of other virtues clustered around it — qualities such as *pudicita* (self-regulation in the area of sexual lust) and *frugalitas* (moderation in spending). The manly man in Roman society was not given to excess, especially in the area of sexuality. As the famous Roman orator Cicero once put it, 'the whole point is to be master of yourself' (*Tusc* 2.22.53). If you couldn't control yourself, then you were regarded as *parum virile*, as unmanly. For the Roman man, discipline was accordingly essential. If a man wanted to be truly healthy — offering a fine, inspiring example to his sons and to others — then he needed to discipline his thinking and his life.

The Roman poet Juvenal hit the nail on the head when he effectively translated the Greek version of *temperantia (sophrosyne)* as *mens sana in corpora sano* — 'a healthy mind in a healthy body.'

For the Roman man, disciplining your mind and disciplining your body went hand-in-hand. An athletic physique was clear evidence that a man had learned the art of self-restraint. An obese physique was ample evidence to the contrary. The manly man in Roman society was accordingly someone who controlled base emotions, like lust, greed and anger, and regulated his eating and exercise — which is perhaps one reason why statues of the Roman Emperor Augustus always portray him in his early life (when he was young and virile) rather than aged 50-70+. Augustus — managing his PR with the astuteness of a modern day Prime Minister — ensured that people only ever saw him at his most manly.

This brings us neatly to Caesar Augustus and the issue of *temperantia*. If we take just one facet of this virtue — self-restraint in the area of lust — it is interesting to note how Augustus attempted to regulate sexual passions, and it is also interesting to observe the gap between Augustus the public figure and Augustus the private man.

It is well known that Augustus became horrified by the amount of sexual immorality in the Rome and its provinces at the time of his great social reforms in the 20s AD and thereafter. He was appalled by the amount of adultery and the consequent weakening of the family unit in Roman society. How could Roman society in its present, decadent form offer a functional model to the rest of the world, much of it now under Roman rule?

In 18-17 BC, Augustus turned his attention to the reform of

marriage. Among the elite classes, fewer and fewer people were getting married and fewer and fewer children were being born. Augustus therefore enacted laws which encouraged marriage and having children, and which also treated adultery as a crime punishable by exile and even death.

These attempts at social reform were poorly received and in fact they backfired against Augustus himself when he was forced by his own legislation to send his daughter Julia into exile for committing adultery. In the end, this legislation was not taken seriously and had to be repealed.

There were a number of reasons why Augustus' marriage laws were doomed. The first had to do with a historic, low view of marriage among Roman men. Perhaps the most famous expression of this cynicism came from Quintus Caecilius Metellus Macedonicus: 'If we could survive without a wife, citizens of Rome, all of us would do without that nuisance, but since nature has so decreed that we cannot manage comfortably with them, nor live in any way without them, we must plan for our lasting preservation rather than our temporary pleasure.'

The second had to do with the draconian nature of some of the legislation. Celibate males of marriageable age who refused to marry were denied their inheritances and barred from the public games. The same was true for young widows who did not want to remarry. Such dictatorial measures denied people their basic human rights and were bound to cause resentment and resistance.

Perhaps the biggest problem however was the example of the one who promoted it — Augustus. In the year 40 BC Augustus (at that time known as Octavian) married Scribonia. His daughter Julia was born in 39 BC. In 38 BC, however, Augustus fell in love with a woman called Livia, who was already married. She had a son (Tiberius) and was pregnant again. Augustus forced her to divorce her husband, divorced his wife, and married Livia. Although this marriage lasted 52 years, its beginnings were not admirable. Furthermore, Augustus and Livia failed to produce any offspring and Augustus was known to take mistresses from the girls serving in the imperial household. Such an inconsistency was bound to bring his legislation into disrepute and cause many Roman men not to take it seriously.

All this led to an unhappy legacy. In effect, Augustus' marriage reforms were insufficient to change peoples' behaviour. While they may have offered some kind of legal restraints to peoples' conduct, they did not nor could not change peoples' hearts. Legislation on its own can never achieve this, especially when those promoting and enacting it are known not to possess the necessary integrity to lend such laws the credibility they need. Augustus' legacy in this area was not a good one. Most of his marriage legislation was either repealed or fell into disuse.

Augustus' legacy within the imperial line after him was not a happy one either. Many of Augustus' successors failed to live up to a high ethical norm in the area of marriage and sexual morality.

Chief among the culprits was the Emperor Nero who, according to the Roman historian Suetonius, was guilty of 'acts of wantonness, lust, extravagance, avarice and cruelty.'

Nero was particularly prone to engaging in acts of sexual immorality with married women and freeborn boys, both of which were off limits to Roman men. Such vices revealed an unmanly softness because they represent the very opposite of self-restraint, of *temperantia*. Coleen Conway explains why:

'Self-mastery was discussed in terms of mastery of the passions, especially lust. Giving in to lustful desire was an indication of sliding down the scale from male to female, since unbridled sexual passion was viewed as a feminine characteristic. In addition, virtues such as courage, honour, justice and scorn of luxury were also important indicators of masculinity. Lack of these qualities suggested softness and effeminacy.'

Conway's comments come from a fascinating article entitled 'Behold the Man', subtitled 'Masculine Christology and the Fourth Gospel.' In this article she looks at how Jesus is portrayed as manly in the Gospel of John.

This brings us once again to the differences between Christ and Caesar.

There is no doubt that Jesus practiced what he preached in his self-restraint. Here is Conway again, 'in terms of lustful passion, there is no indication in any of the Gospel traditions of Jesus being tempted by sexual passion, so there seems little room to comment on his accomplishments in this area... '

Conway goes on to look at scenes from the Fourth Gospel, beginning with the interaction between Jesus and the Samaritan woman in John 4.4-42. She rightly shows how this whole story is told using a particular genre of storytelling used in the Hebrew Scriptures. This story form is known as the betrothal scene and had a number of common features: a man and a woman meet at a well, they talk, they draw water from the well, they eat a feast with the woman's family, and then they become engaged. Isaac, Jacob and Moses all experience such betrothals. To the Jewish reader of the fourth gospel — familiar with such stories in the Hebrew Bible — there can only be one conclusion: the Jewish man Jesus is about to enter into an intimate relationship with a despised Samaritan woman.

And yet, no betrothal takes place. There is no hint of a romantic relationship. As Coleen Conway puts it: 'Even while Jesus skirts close to the matter of the woman's sexuality, in the end he speaks only of spiritual matters.'

This is all the more interesting when we remember how Jesus conducts himself at the garden tomb after his resurrection. There he meets Mary Magdalene, a female disciple who held him in the highest regard and loved him dearly. As Conway shows, some of the behaviour of Mary Magdalene in this story has echoes of the behaviour of the woman searching for her male lover in the Song of Songs. Yet, as Conway correctly notes,

'Jesus sounds nothing like the male lover from the poem as he warns her not to touch him (John 20.17).'

What all this shows is that even when stories seem tailor-made for passionate and romantic associations, these expectations are not fulfilled. Jesus exercises perfect self-restraint. He is the very epitome of manly *temperantia*.

What this leaves us with is accordingly an example of great moral integrity. Jesus' ethics — the ethics, that is, of the Kingdom of God — represent a much more demanding and rigorous level of honesty than that provided by his contemporaries, especially the Pharisees. When it came to lust, he made it clear that it wasn't enough simply to avoid performing immoral acts. He said that lusting after another woman in your heart was the same as committing adultery. Therefore, what happens internally is as important as what happens externally — in a person's actions.

In all of this, Jesus does not pass legislation, enacting civil laws that restrain people from committing adultery. He first of all offers an example in his own life. Unlike Caesar, Christ practiced what he preached. In all his dealings with women, he established internal boundaries in his heart and mind which in turn produced external borders in his relating. These borders allowed Jesus to express full compassion towards the women he met, who therefore felt liberated rather than exploited. This makes Jesus a thoroughly inspiring example to Christian men.

Secondly, Jesus' own restraint was not just a matter of human willpower alone. He was helped by the Holy Spirit in his behaviour. We know this because the Apostle Paul was later to describe 'self-control' as a 'fruit of the Holy Spirit.' Jesus — the quintessential Spirit-filled man — exercised restraint not only because he made the right choices but also because the Holy Spirit empowered him in his decision-making.

What, then, are the implications for Christian men?

The most obvious implication is that *temperantia* is a noble attribute of manhood and masculinity but it needs — as with all the other Roman qualities of *virtu* — to be radically reshaped in the light of the example of Jesus.

Christian men are called to conform to the image of Christ not Caesar. What does this mean?

First of all it means we are called to make sure that our inner life is under the rule of God. Christian men need to place their passions — all their passions, not just sexual passion — under the reign of Christ the Lord. He offers men a compelling example of purity and integrity. We must try to be as honest and as holy as the Master.

Secondly, no man needs to go it alone in the exercise of self-restraint. If he is in Christ he has the help of Christ — the greatest example of masculinity in human history. He also has the help of the Holy Spirit, whose fruit is 'self-control.' This means that we have supernatural help; it is not just a matter of human effort (though that is vital too).

It is also imperative to remember that we not only have the help of the Holy Spirit, we also have the help of other Christian men. Jesus established a band of brothers when he called the Twelve. This forever sanctifies the values of friendship and accountability for Christian males and undermines all purely individualistic models of sanctification.

Thirdly, we should note that in spite of Dan Brown's claims in The Da Vinci Code, Jesus Christ did not marry Mary Magdalene. He didn't marry anyone. This means that it is by no means a second best life if a Christian man chooses to be single and not to marry and have children. Unlike Caesar Augustus, Jesus does not legislate that a male disciple must marry and have a family if they are going to be honoured and useful members of his kingdom. Jesus shows from his own life and example that being unmarried is just as honourable.

What matters in the end therefore is not that a man is married or unmarried. What matters is that in either context — that of singleness or marriage — a man is conformed to the image of Christ and thinks and acts like Jesus.

This means embracing the virtue of temperantia, understood as the kind of self-control modelled by Jesus and empowered by the Holy Spirit.

And it means embracing this manly virtue not just in the area of sexual passions but in all the passions — including for example greed and anger.

As ever, the virtues of the Kingdom are far more demanding and yet inspiring than the virtues of the Empire.

Chapter 5:

GENEROSITY

The Roman man was a person who was meant to live without excess. He chose not to overspend on the luxuries of life and to live simply. This was seen as a sign of *temperantia* at work. It showed he was self-controlled.

Of course sometimes frugality can result in a miserable and miserly temperament. An example in literature would be Ebenezer Scrooge, who hoarded his wealth, lived austerely and never gave his resources away in the service of others.

The Roman man was not encouraged to display this kind of meanness. Rather, he was expected to exhibit the virtue of generosity in giving. While living simply himself, he was supposed to be generous to others.

This brings us to the fifth virtue of the manly man, *liberalitas*, understood to mean 'generosity in giving.' The Roman Emperor, as the epitome of Roman manhood and masculinity, was supposed to exhibit this virtue more than anyone else. He was expected to show forth in public an inspiring combination of frugality and liberality. The way the Emperors chose to do this varied greatly but those who lived modestly and gave generously were always lauded and were often held up as a model of manhood for all aspiring males.

Very often imperial coins would actually record the number of occasions on which an Emperor made generous donations of either money or grain. These coins would contain an image of the goddess *Liberalitas* holding two items: a counting board for the distribution of coins and a cornucopia representing the distribution of corn, grain and wheat.

This brings us to the Emperor Augustus. In what ways did Caesar Augustus model in public life this combination of frugality (the virtue of a simple lifestyle) and liberality (the virtue of imperial munificence)?

Let's begin with Augustus' simplicity of life.

Augustus was very keen for the people of Rome to know that he practised what he preached — especially during all his social and moral reforms — so he chose to live modestly and even austerely when in Rome. According to the Roman historian Suetonius, for forty years Augustus lived in a house on the Palatine which was far from palatial. In fact, Suetonius remarks that Augustus' home was notable for its modesty. He says, it was 'remarkable neither for size nor for elegance; the courts being supported by squat columns of peperino stone, and the living rooms innocent of marble or elaborately tasselled floors.'

All this suggests that in Rome Augustus appeared to live a life of relative austerity and simplicity, which is what Suetonius and others indicate. In fact, Suetonius says of Augustus' domestic furniture that it 'would hardly be fit for a private citizen.'

At the same time, Augustus was extremely generous. Out of his immense wealth he gave extraordinary amounts of money towards the rebuilding of the city of Rome and the needs of the Roman people.

Where did Augustus' enormous personal wealth come from? The following represents a general summary of the sources:

1. His inheritance from Julius Caesar
2. Legacies he received from Roman citizens
3. Profits from the Civil War (against Antony and Cleopatra)
4. Income from large estates in the Empire
5. The treasures of Egypt

With this kind of wealth, Augustus would sometimes top up the coffers in Rome. The Aerarium (or treasury) was based at the temple of Saturn in the Roman Forum. It was overseen by two praetors and it sometimes ran low on funds. In these situations, Augustus would give from his own wealth for buildings to be refurbished, roads to be built (the *curia viarum*), grain to be supplied, soldiers to be paid and extensive farmland to be purchased (especially for retiring veterans of the Roman legions). When the treasury ran low or the Senate was uncooperative, Augustus — as the wealthiest man in Rome — would simply exercise *liberalitas*. The primary way in which the Emperor Augustus exercised generosity was therefore in domestic affairs — in his support for the people and the infrastructure of the city of Rome.

But there was also another manifestation of his generosity – one which tended to be seen in foreign rather than domestic affairs. This had to do with the virtue of *clementia* or mercy extended towards some of the enemies of Rome.

Now it is true that Augustus was capable of exercising brute and even brutal force when dealing with his enemies. We shouldn't forget for example that he had Mark Antony's name erased from all public records. At the same time, Augustus realised that long-term peace in conquered territories would sometimes best be achieved through exercising clemency with one's enemies so that they in turn could prove reliable and wise rulers of Rome's new territories.

In this respect we should briefly note another example of Augustus' noteworthy *prudentia* or strategic foresight. He recognised that irrational, punitive force against a conquered enemy could mar the long-term maintenance of pax *Romana*.

Plutarch has a memorable anecdote which confirms Augustus' *prudentia* here. He writes that Augustus once heard that Alexander the Great had been baffled by what to do next after all his global, military conquests. Apparently the Emperor had stated his own surprise. He was reported to have said, 'I am surprised that the king did not recognise that a far more demanding task than winning an empire is putting it into order once you have won it.'

This desire to rebuild nations after conquering them was therefore at the root of Augustus' exercise of *clementia*. As he wrote, 'as victor I spared all the citizens who sought pardon. As for foreign nations, those which I was able safely to forgive, I preferred to preserve rather than destroy' (*Res Gestae* 3)

At home and away, therefore, Augustus exhibited *liberalitas*. In his dealings with his own people, he gave immeasurable amounts to their welfare. In his dealings with his enemies, he sometimes showed great clemency.

Philo says this of Augustus in his eulogy:

'This is Caesar, who calmed the storms which were raging in every direction, who healed the common diseases which were afflicting both Greeks and barbarians... This is he who did not only loosen but utterly abolish the bonds in which the whole of the habitable world was previously bound and weighed down. This is he who destroyed both the evident and the unseen wars which arose from the attacks of robbers. This is he who rendered the sea free from the vessels of pirates, and filled it with Merchantmen... This is he who gave freedom to every city, who brought disorder into order, who civilized and made obedient and harmonious, nations which before his time were unsociable, hostile, and brutal. This is ... the guardian of peace, the distributor to every man of what was suited to him, the man who proffered to all the citizens favors with the most ungrudging liberality, who never once in his whole life concealed or reserved for himself anything that was good or excellent.'

[Legat 21.145-147]

Notice Philo's celebration of Augustus' 'ungrudging liberality' in the final sentence. According to Philo, Augustus offered the

Roman Empire a public picture of virtue. He lived a life of personal frugalitas or austerity (never reserving for himself anything that was good or excellent) and public *liberalitas* (distributing to every man what was good for him'

How, then, is *liberalitas* evidenced in the life of Jesus of Nazareth? The answer is in at least two ways. Jesus' showed *liberalitas* in his miracles and he showed it equally in his mercy.

Let's look first of all at miracles.

While it is true that Jesus, being God in flesh on the earth, had all the material resources of the planet to share with those in need, his generosity was seen first and foremost in his provision of spiritual rather than material riches.

In this respect, Jesus was never guilty of what could be laid at the feet of Caesar Augustus – the charge that he was able to be generous to his own people because he had first robbed foreign nations. New Testament scholar Jerome H. Neyrey underlines this when he describes Jesus as a benefactor who was 'able to increase the amount of goods, not by taking from others (i.e., spoils), but by divine benefaction that expands the supply and enriches all. In this, Jesus stands head and shoulders over other benefactors of the world, who must despoil many to benefit a few.'

That is right. The source of Jesus' extravagant munificence was not some conquered earthly power in an Empire. Rather, Jesus gave out of the indescribable riches of the Kingdom of God. He gave out of heaven's treasury.

In light of this we should not be surprised to learn that the *liberalitas* of Jesus of Nazareth was exhibited in the way he brought the resources of heaven to those experiencing hell on earth. Jesus demonstrated the power of God through healing the sick, delivering the oppressed, cleansing the lepers and raising the dead. In short, he revealed his liberality first of all through miracles.

In one particularly revealing and memorable episode, Jesus feeds five thousand hungry men after he had been teaching them on a mountain in the run up to the Jewish Feast of Passover.

Now to understand the full importance of this story we must have a grasp of the historical and social context of this miracle – and in particular one of the means used by the Roman army to enforce *Pax Romana* in their conquered territories. One of their time-honoured methods was to impose a bread rationing system in their occupied lands. While giving their legionaries a full daily ration of bread, the indigenous and conquered males would be given only a paltry amount. In other words, the Empire ensured that their soldiers were given their daily bread to keep them strong. At the same time, it ensured that the men these soldiers had conquered were given a tiny amount of bread to keep them weak. If they were weak, they would be unlikely to mount an insurrection against Rome.

It is in this context that Jesus performs one of his best known miracles when he takes five loaves and two fishes and multiplies them supernaturally so that all 5000 men (and the additional women and children) are fully fed and satisfied.

What happens next, at least according to John's version of the story, is fascinating. John tells us that Jesus immediately withdrew after this miracle because he knew that the people wanted to make him king 'by force.' (John 6.15)

Why did the people want to do this? It was because Christ was providing what the Empire was denying them — a full ration of daily bread. With Christ the King at their head — a King who can multiply bread — they would be strong indeed!

And so Jesus withdraws and he does so because his generosity is not politically motivated. It is simply the unmerited, miraculous generosity of heaven displayed to those in need on the earth.

If Jesus shows *liberalitas* through miracles, he also reveals it through mercy.

This is definitely seen in the way Jesus looks down from the Cross at those tormenting and torturing him — including representatives of the Roman Empire — and says, 'Father, forgive them, for they know not what they do.'

Nowhere is the marked difference between Augustus' mercy and Jesus' mercy more visible than right here.

From the Roman point of view, the exercise of clemency was really motivated by a kind of enlightened self-interest. You showed mercy to your enemies when it was to your benefit — in terms of long-term political welfare — to do so.

In this respect, Roman clemency was exercised strategically and occasionally, not thoughtlessly and frequently. Any Emperor that exercised clemency without due care was showing weakness, not strength.

In Jesus' life, however, clemency was not motivated by enlightened self-interest. Rather, his mercy was relational not political. He extended mercy because of the Father's great love, not because it was a means to an end.

So Jesus' liberality is seen in the way he blesses people with the miraculous resources of the Kingdom of heaven and the startling, merciful virtues of the heart of his Father in heaven. Jesus was lavishly generous in his display of miracles and mercy. This was not strategic imperial munificence. It was grace. It was the liberal, undeserved and prodigious generosity of God's unsearchable riches.

What are the implications for Christian men?

The first miracle performed by the earliest church is described in Acts chapters 3 and 4 and it is revealing. There we read a story about the Apostles, Peter and John, and their encounter with a lame man at the Beautiful Gate in Jerusalem.

Luke records the opening of the story thus in Acts 3:1-3:

One day Peter and John were going up to the temple at the time of prayer-at three in the afternoon. Now a man crippled from birth was being carried to the temple gate called Beautiful, where he was put every day to beg from those going into the temple courts. When he saw Peter and John about to enter, he asked them for money.

Here is a story about two men in the fledgling Christian church after Pentecost. They are Jewish men, as can be seen by the fact that they are about to go to prayer at one of the three hours for prayer in first century Judaism. On their way to the meeting, they are hailed by a man asking for money. As the old pun goes, 'a man without the use of his legs asks for alms.' In fact, as we are about to find out, it is legs not alms that are going to be the focus here. What are Peter and John to do? They have seen their Master Jesus many times stop what he was doing in order to meet the needs of just one desperate person. Will they prioritize the value of a solitary life above that of their own plans? The answer is of course yes. Luke records that Peter fastens his eyes upon the man who has been lame since birth and says, 'silver or gold I have none, but what I have I give you' — and the man is miraculously healed so that he leaps for joy.

Here we see the *liberalitas* of the Christian manly man. The Christian man may not have much in terms of material resources. Peter and John certainly didn't. Peter's confession is hardly one in which he parades his wealth. He says, 'silver and gold I have none.' In other words, 'I'm living a frugal, simple life without excess and extravagance. In fact, I don't have two coins to rub together!' But then he goes on to add these words, 'what I have I give you.' This statement contains what are arguably the six most important words for Christian men in the whole of the Book of Acts. 'What I have I give you.' What Peter has — and John the Apostle too — is heavenly resources. They have the resources given as a result of the outpouring of the Holy Spirit on the Day of Pentecost. They have the supernatural power and love of God working in and through them.

For a Christian man, giving much depends on receiving much. You cannot give what you do not have. Therefore it is imperative for Christian men to be filled and to go on being filled with the Holy Spirit. It is vital for a Christian man to be able to know 'what I have.'

Beyond that, every Christian man must be prepared to wed this anointing of power with a heart of compassion — with a willingness to show mercy to the marginalised and invisible people of society. In other words, it is vital for Christian men to be able to go on to say, 'I give you.'

Whenever we expend ourselves in this virtue of generosity, the Kingdom of God is extended. Its borders are not advanced through military might or material riches. They are enlarged through supernatural power and unselfish clemency.

Once again we see the huge contrast between Christ and Caesar and between Kingdom and Empire.

BEHOLD THE MAN

Chapter 6:

FAITHFULNESS

One of the men most revered by Romans in the ancient world was a certain Lucius Quinctius Cincinnatus (519-460 BC). He was one of the heroes of the early history of Rome and became a model of Roman virtue.

Cincinnatus had at one time been a wealthy member of the ruling classes and had held the office of consul *suffectus* in Rome but as a result of his son being condemned to death he had now fallen on hard times and was looking after a little farm.

In spite of this, he was still highly respected for his wisdom by everyone who knew him; whenever there was a dispute or a dilemma locally, his neighbours would invariably say, 'go and tell Cincinnatus. He will help you.'

One day, as the story goes, he was busy ploughing a field when five senatorial messengers turned up from Rome, covered in dust and no small amount of blood. They were hot foot from the city and clearly anxious.

At their request Cincinnatus' wife Racilia brought her husband's consul's toga from the house and draped it on him. The senators immediately hailed him as their Dictator before explaining why they were there.

Cincinnatus heard that Rome was in catastrophic danger from the tribes of the Aequi, Sabines, and Volsci, and that Consul Minucius Esquilinus and his army were trapped in a mountain pass.

The Senate had been in a panic when someone had said, 'go and tell Cincinnatus. He will help you.' In the process, Horatius Pulvilius nominated Cincinnatus as *Magister Populi*, or 'Master of the People' for six months.

As Cincinnatus listened he was now in a quandary. Both he and his family were totally dependent on the produce of their land for their very survival. To leave the fields unploughed would mean great hardship and possibly even death.

But Cincinnatus' commitment to Rome was unwavering and so he agreed to go with the men on a boat across the Tiber whereupon he was greeted by his three sons and the Senators and given several *lictors* for his personal protection.

Cincinnatus that same day raised an army at the *Campus Martius* and marched towards the enemy, engaging them at the Battle of Mons Algidus. He led the foot soldiers in person while his second in command, Tarquitus, led the cavalry.

The Aequi were taken completely by surprise by this sudden, two pronged attack and were cut to pieces. Their leader, Gracchus Cloelius, and his officers were put in chains and the war came to an end.

Within a fortnight Cincinnatus had restored peace. But far from continuing in office, he immediately abdicated his absolute authority and went back to ploughing his field. In all, he had been Rome's leader for just sixteen days.

Roman men at the time of Augustus (and indeed for centuries before) idolised Cincinnatus because they saw in him the very apex of the kind of civic, public virtue that they regarded as essential for the Roman manly man.

In particular, Cincinnatus became an example of *fides* — faithfulness to the gods, to the good of Rome and to the cause of Rome. His loyalty had been put to the test when his son had been condemned but he remained faithful.

In fact, Cincinnatus had been so loyal and true that when he was faced with the choice of providing for his family or saving Rome he chose the latter and went off to fight against Rome's enemies.

As such, he became the archetype of that faithfulness to the cause of Rome that led to active, self-sacrificial and noble service. Cincinnatus, in short, became an example of the kind of virtu that was to typify Roman men.

As the Roman historian Livy — contemporary with Augustus — was later to say:

'It is worthwhile for those who disdain all human things for money, and who suppose that there is no room either for great honour or virtue, except where wealth is found, to listen to his story.' (3.26)

Fides was accordingly a highly regarded quality in Roman society. If a man wanted to develop *virtu* — in other words, become a 'manly man' — then he had better emulate Cincinnatus and be true to Rome and true to his word.

Caesar Augustus was a man characterised by *fides*. He was true to his word. If, as the *princeps* (the first citizen) of Rome he promised something, then he would deliver on it. 'I am a man of my word', he would say.

Similarly, Augustus' unwavering loyalty to Rome was never in question. He was faithful in his active and self-sacrificial service to the people of Rome, Italy and the Provinces. He was a man of true *fides*.

Augustus' faithfulness to the gods is something we have already noted in the chapter on piety. But he was also loyal to the 'worthies of old', the ancient heroes of Rome, whom he venerated in statues and inscriptions.

And he was faithful to his people. So when the Senate insisted that Augustus accept the title 'Father of your Country', Suetonius reports that Augustus wept as he thanked them for the fulfilment of his highest hopes.

No question then — *fides* was highly valued in the Roman Empire. A man could never attain greatness in public affairs without loyal, active service to the cause of Rome and without being true to his word and trustworthy.

In what way, then, do we see *fides* exhibited and redefined in the life of Jesus Christ?

In Jesus we see a different kind of faithfulness and indeed a different expression of it for Jesus' faithfulness was not to the Empire of Rome but to the Father's will and it was not expressed in military conquests but in his self-sacrificial death.

In Jesus' life too, faithfulness was his path to greatness, and yet what is surprising is the fact that he should be venerated when his faithfulness was not expressed in military triumph but in a shameful, ignominious slave's death.

What is equally startling is the fact that Jesus did not attain greatness from the advantageous platform of a membership of the privileged, elite classes (as Augustus had) but from the fields of Galilee.

In fact, we should always remember that Jesus was not born within a royal house or a prestigious estate but grew up within the confines of a carpenter's house in the small town of Nazareth and was part of the peasant class in Galilee.

How then did this man come out of obscurity and inscribe into the human race a completely new understanding of faithfulness?

How did he redefine the path to greatness for all men?

What was it in his teaching and his life that brought about such a radical revision of the understanding of virtue?

Jesus' life and teaching showed that greatness meant serving others not one's self. He said, 'greater love has no one than this, than to lay down one's life for his friends.' (John 15.13)

Jesus lived in a 'hierarchical world where every person was classified according to conventional notions of wealth, power, status... Few males had the opportunity to fulfil the ideal stereotype of masculinity.'

Yet Jesus Christ, a peasant from Nazareth, crossed the boundary lines of his society and turned masculinity, the honour of manhood, the virtue and complexity of being a man, on its head.

Jerome Neyrey suggests that, 'Jesus redefines the prevailing male value of honour ... an honour that comes not from nobility or martial prowess but from a grace, a giving up [of] power to empower others.'

In such a redefinition, true masculinity has no right to take a life. Quite the opposite – a true man has the power to give a life, his own life, and this was how Jesus demonstrated his revisionist masculinity.

In Graeco-Roman philosophy, 'the higher the societal status that one achieved, the more masculine one became and vice versa'. There is nothing of this in Jesus' lifestyle or in the ethics of the Kingdom of God.

In fact, Jesus turns this cultural elitism upside down and effectively says that 'the 'greatest in the kingdom of heaven is not the ruler or leader but a young child...the great ones and the first should be like Jesus, the servant of all.'

Jerome Neyrey elaborates: 'Jesus may seem not to conform to the gender stereotype when he demands his followers that they (1) eschew male games of physical and sexual aggression to gain honour; (2) vacate the public forum to perform their piety; (3) endure shameful actions, such as ostracization; (4) forsake family wealth; and (5) become lowly and serve others, but these shameful actions actually become the way to honour in the eyes of God and Jesus.'

Jesus' greatness therefore came from a road of self-emptying not egotistical ambition. He acknowledged that the cup of suffering was too much to bear, but in full obedience, surrendered to the will of his heavenly Father

In the process, Jesus unveiled the masquerade and facade of Graeco-Roman masculinity; he gave up 'gender power' and showed not only man but humankind how to suffer shame on behalf of another. He was therefore given 'honour of one who is mighty and great, because he exposed himself to death. He was counted among those who were sinners. He bore the sins of many and interceded for sinners.' (Isaiah 53.12)

Jesus Christ therefore exhibits *fides* but it is not the kind of *fides* that was seen in Augustus. For Jesus, the path to greatness was a path of self-emptying, humiliation, torture, and execution — all performed by the employees of Rome.

Caesar Augustus, an illustrious member of Rome's elite class, served the cause of Rome faithfully through military and governmental prowess. Jesus Christ, a humble carpenter from Galilee, served his Father by dying on a Roman Cross.

What, then, are the implications for Christian men?

The answer is simple: we are called to be conformed to the image of Christ not Caesar and remember that faithfulness — especially expressed through self-sacrifice and humility — is the path to greatness.

Remember what the church in Smyrna — forged in the context of the Roman Empire and on the furnace of persecution — is told by the Ascended Jesus. 'Be faithful even to the point of death and I will give you the crown of life' (Revelation 2.10)

Notice the phrase 'crown of life' (*stephanos*). This is the laurel wreath crown given by the Roman Emperor to the winning athlete at the Games, or to a victorious general on his return to Rome.

To the man who is faithful to the very end — in the revisionist understanding of *fides* exhibited by the life and death of Jesus — there is the promise of a victory crown, and when it comes to promises Jesus' is true to His Word.

He is 'faithful and true.'

So Christian men can take heart that even though their path to greatness may be tough in the extreme, in the end they will be declared to be a champion on the fields of heaven.

Perhaps a story would form the most apt conclusion.

In the ancient Roman Empire, many Christians refused to serve in the imperial armies, finding it was in conflict with their baptismal vows and the teaching and example of Jesus.

In The Apostolic Tradition of St. Hippolytus of Rome, written in the second century and attributed to one of the first Bishops of Rome, renunciation of killing is a precondition of baptism: 'A soldier under authority shall not kill a man. If he is ordered to, he shall not carry out the order, nor shall he take the oath. If he is unwilling, let him be rejected. He who has the power of the sword or is a magistrate of a city who wears the purple, let him cease or be rejected. Catechumens or believers, who want to become soldiers, should be rejected, because they have despised God.' (Canon XVI: On Professions)

But what about soldiers who were converted to Christianity? One could not simply walk away from the Roman army. To be a soldier was like any other trade: it was not done for a few years but throughout adulthood, until one was too old or infirm to continue.

Some were fortunate — their duties did not require the exercise of deadly force. A few — for example, Martin of Tours — were able to obtain a special discharge. Some, however, took the path of martyrdom.

Marcellus the Centurion, after some years of army service, found he could no longer continue in military obedience. One day in AD 298, during the reign of the Emperor Diocletian, Marcellus's unit in northern Africa was celebrating the pagan emperor's birthday with a party. Suddenly Marcellus rose before the banqueters and denounced such celebrations as heathen. Casting off his military insignia, he cried out, 'I serve Jesus Christ the eternal King. I will no longer serve your emperors and I scorn to worship your gods of wood and stone, which are deaf and dumb idols.'

Marcellus was immediately arrested for breach of discipline. At his trial, he admitted that he had done that of which he was accused. He declared that it is 'not right for a Christian man, who serves the Lord Christ, to serve in the armies of the world.' Found guilty, he was immediately beheaded. According to the ancient testimonies, he died in great peace of mind, asking God to bless the judge who had condemned him.

Now that is an example of an otherworldly *fides* — a faithfulness that comes from heaven and is exemplified supremely in the life and death of the Man from Heaven, Jesus Christ.

Chapter 7:

LOVE OF TRUTH

One of the most dramatic 'face-offs' in the Gospels occurs when Pontius Pilate, the Roman governor in Jerusalem, is compelled to judge and then condemn to death the one described as 'the King of the Jews.'

In the Johannine account of this confrontation (John 18.28-19.12), the sense of drama is increased by the way that John the storyteller brilliantly re-describes this 'face-off' in seven scenes. These seven scenes alternate between spaces outside and inside the Praetorium. The first episode involves Pilate going outside to meet the Jewish leaders. The second involves him going inside to interrogate Jesus, and so on.

The centre-piece of this drama is the fourth scene (i.e. the middle scene of the seven) where Pilate has Jesus severely flogged. When he sees Jesus he declares, 'behold the man!' In Latin he may have said, *'Ecce Vir!'*

Be that as it may, our focus here is actually on something else Pilate says, this time at the end of the second scene (inside the Praetorium) where he asks Jesus, 'what is truth?' There is of course great irony here. Pontius Pilate asks 'what is truth?' But he is standing in front of the man who has described himself as 'the Truth' (John 14.6). Pilate asks the incarnation of truth for a definition of truth!

It is not this often made point that I want to emphasize here, however. Instead, I want to suggest that Pontius Pilate's question is an expression of a value that was very important to a Roman man — namely the love of truth.

In Roman society, one of the qualities that had to characterize the man of virtu — in other words, 'the manly man' — was a deep respect and love for veritas, or truth. Pilate is no exception. He asks Jesus, 'Quid est veritas?'

For Pilate this is not a metaphysical or a philosophical issue. This is a very practical issue to do with right governance in the public sphere. For Pilate, veritas can roughly be translated as 'integrity.'

Integrity in leadership is a vital quality in Roman culture. No man could ever be truly fit to lead if he was one thing in private and quite another in public. The Romans were quick to spot such inconsistencies.

For Pilate, then, the issue is one of transparency. He's asking, 'what is reality in this case that I'm adjudicating?' Are the chief priests being real? Is this man Jesus being real? Where is veritas to be found in this situation?

In light of this, we might be a little less hard on Pilate. It may be true that he fails to spot that Jesus is the Truth in person, or *Veritas* incarnate, but who among us would have readily understood that on such a first and intense encounter?

We believe that Pilate was simply responding as a Roman man in this situation. For him, reality and integrity were important. So, as a lover of truth, all he is saying here is this: 'Where is integrity to be seen in this case before me?'

What, then, of Caesar Augustus? Was he a man who loved truth? In what ways did he exhibit the levels of integrity required of a manly man in the public sphere? Was he a good role model for men in pursuit of *veritas*?

The answer has to be no.

Let's take just two examples of the inconsistencies that constantly undermined Augustus' character and to a degree his leadership.

The first example we want to take is one that we've hinted at already. In our chapter on *temperantia* we pointed out that Augustus' legislation against adultery was disregarded by many because of his own lack of integrity in this area of his life.

We only have to conduct a cursory reading of Suetonius' account of Augustus' reign (told in *The Lives of the Twelve Caesars*) to discover that there were widely reported instances of impropriety.

Here are a few excerpts:

'That he was given to adultery not even his friends deny, although it is true that they excuse it as committed not from passion but from policy, the more readily to get track of his adversaries' designs through the women of their households.'

'Mark Antony charged him, besides his hasty marriage with Livia, with taking the wife of an ex-consul from her husband's dining-room before his very eyes into a bed-chamber, and bringing her back to the table with her hair in disorder and her ears glowing.'

'His friends acted as his panders, and stripped and inspected matrons and well-grown girls, as if Toranius the slave-dealer were putting them up for sale.'

'He could not dispose of the charge of lustfulness and they say that even in his later years he was fond of deflowering maidens, who were brought together for him from all quarters, even by his own wife.'

While it is hard to know just how much this is a matter of idle gossip, the truth is that there's usually no smoke without fire, and this 'charge of lustfulness' was well known in Rome and also affected Augustus' judgments. Indeed, there was one famous occasion when Augustus was presiding as a judge, attempting to distribute *iustititia* or 'justice' in a situation involving a young man who had taken as his wife a married woman with whom he had committed adultery. This was a very embarrassing moment for Augustus because this is exactly what he had done when he married Livia in 38 BC. He therefore took a while to recover his composure but when he did, all he could find to say was, 'let us turn our minds to the future so that nothing of this kind can happen again.'

Augustus was therefore known to lack *veritas* in his personal morality and all this undermined his attempts to push through marriage reforms. There was simply a lack of *veritas* in relation to his self-control. As Anthony Everitt pithily remarks in his excellent biography of Augustus, 'moral campaigns are most likely to succeed if led by someone who has nothing with which to reproach himself.'

The second area where Augustus lacked *veritas* is in his accommodation. In the chapter on *temperantia*, we mentioned that his house in Rome was modestly appointed and poorly furnished. This implied that Augustus led a simple lifestyle and that he embodied the value of austerity — so admired by Roman men. Indeed, the impression we have given thus far is that Augustus was far more concerned with bettering the city than he was his house. While he left Rome decked in marble, his own home was notable (at least in Suetonius' account) for its lack of marble. On the surface of it at least, this appears to point to a commendable degree of self-control in the purchase and decorating of his homes.

But all this once again masks the real story. While his home in Rome was relatively austere, this was in fact a public facade. In reality, Augustus had another villa which was far away from the public eye. This home – a truly palatial residence – was especially built for him on the island of Pandateria, about thirty miles west of Naples. This tiny island was turned into Augustus' private getaway. It had a purpose built small harbour, servant's quarters, fountains and colonnades, seats and stairways, and a large villa, which Everitt describes as follows:

'The main house was reached by walking up from the valley to where it stood on a high promontory. The building was shaped like a horseshoe, with a garden in the middle, and was perched on precipitous cliffs. At the tip of the promontory a viewing platform offered an uninterrupted panorama of sky and sea. Here was secret spendour, where the *princeps* could entertain his intimate circle in undisturbed privacy.'

It seems then that Augustus lacked *veritas* in at least two areas of his personal life — marital faithfulness and domestic austerity.

Indeed, one cannot miss the glaring gap between the private man and the public image.

When it comes to Jesus of Nazareth, we once again see a huge difference.

If ever there was a man who was consistent it was Jesus.

If ever there was a man who exhibited reality and transparency, it was Jesus.

If ever there was a man who practiced what he preached, it was Jesus.

If ever there was a man who was the same in private as in public, it was Jesus.

If ever there was a man who showed integrity as a leader, it was Jesus.

Jesus did not preach austerity while living a prosperous life. Rather, he had no home of his own and no possessions. He said that even foxes have holes and birds of the air have nests but the Son of Man has nowhere to lay his head.

When Jesus died he left no houses or palaces, no furniture or possessions, no cash or treasure; he left only the one-piece tunic that he was wearing, for which his four Roman executioners cast lots.

Furthermore, Jesus did not commend marriage and fidelity while himself living a secretly immoral life. In fact, he was the most consistent person who has ever lived — the private and the public wedded together in a startling integrity.

All this highlights something massively significant about the man Christ Jesus and that is the uniqueness of his character. No other leader — including religious leader — has ever lived such a holy life, both internally and externally. Indeed, if ever there was a man who deserved the word 'perfect,' it is Jesus of Nazareth. He was perfect in righteousness, perfect in kindness, perfect in justice, perfect in love.

People made charges against him but none of these stuck. Some criticised him for being demon possessed, others for being a drunkard and a glutton. But in these and every other case, the evidence was never produced and the accusations were regarded as risible.

Jesus Christ is the most credible and trustworthy man who has ever lived.

This is what John the Gospel writer was trying to convey implicitly in his account of Jesus' meeting with the Samaritan woman. Remember what Jesus says to her, 'you've had five husbands and the man you're now living with is not your husband.' How many men does that make? It makes six. But she is now in the presence of a seventh man — Jesus of Nazareth — and seven is the number of perfection in Judaism. It is the number of wholeness and completion.

Jesus is the perfect man. Men and women find their true fulfilment in following him. They find true joy in conforming to the image of Jesus Christ.

So what are the implications for Christian men?

Jesus said, 'be perfect even as your heavenly Father is perfect.' In other words, with the help of the Holy Spirit, grow up to the fullness of the stature of Jesus Christ. Recognize that your full potentiality and maturity as a man are found in relating to Jesus and indeed in imitating Jesus.

For Christian men today, this means cultivating *veritas*. It means becoming lovers of truth and reality, resolving to be the same person in the public sphere as in the private sphere, behind closed doors.

In his highly acclaimed and brilliant book *The Speed of Trust*, Stephen Covey makes a bold, articulate and passionate bid to reinstate trustworthiness as a pivotal virtue in leadership in the public sphere today.

Covey rightly says that character and competence are both essential for effective and high impact leadership, but he also says that we have tended to elevate competence and neglect character – but it is character that should take precedence.

In reality, people will only follow leaders that they trust, hence the title of the book, *The Speed of Trust*. If a leader is seen over time to be utterly trustworthy – in other words to have integrity of character — people will follow fast.

For Covey, then, there is a call for leaders in all walks of life to cultivate the forgotten value of trust and to develop this quality in private and in secret before seeking to demonstrate it in the public arena. As Covey puts it,

'The process of building trust is an interesting one, but it begins with yourself, with what I call self trust, and with your own credibility, your own trustworthiness. If you think about it, it's hard to establish trust with others if you can't trust yourself.'

For Covey, trust is accordingly essential. When the level of trust is low, the speed of an organization slows down and the cost goes up. When the level of trust is high, the speed of an organization goes up and the cost goes down.

How then is trust increased in an organization?

Trust, in Covey's thesis, begins with the individual leader's trustworthiness. Here he talks about the importance of integrity and the vital need that every leader has to ask the question, 'am I congruent?' 'Am I in alignment with my values?'

Beyond that, Covey argues that trust can greatly be enhanced if the following thirteen behaviour patterns are modelled and encouraged by those in leadership:

- Talk straight
- Demonstrate respect
- Create transparency
- Right wrongs
- Show loyalty
- Deliver results
- Get better
- Confront reality

- Clarify expectations
- Practice accountability
- Listen first
- Keep commitments
- Extend trust

Any Christian man who wants to develop both their character as a man and their competence as a leader would do very well to heed Covey's advice and to learn from his own contemporary celebration of *veritas*.

As the world famous evangelist Dr Billy Graham once famously stated, 'the true Christian is someone who is prepared to lend their pet parrot to the town gossip!'

In other words, the real Christian is real.

And the Christian manly man is known for integrity at every level of his life.

This of course is a tough challenge because we tend to behave like the Man of Dust (the First Adam) rather than the Man from Heaven (the Last Adam).

But this is where honesty among men is so important.

Listen to a former Bishop of Edinburgh, who expresses this kind of healing honesty so eloquently:

'This is my dilemma...I am dust and ashes, frail and wayward, a set of pre-determined behavioural responses,...riddled with fears, beset with needs..., the quintessence of dust and unto dust I shall return... But there is something else in me... Dust I may be, but troubled dust, dust that dreams, dust that has strange premonitions of transfiguration, of a glory in store, a destiny prepared, an inheritance that will one day be my own...So my life is stretched out in a painful dialectic between ashes and glory, between weakness and transfiguration. I am a riddle to myself, an exasperating enigma..., this strange duality of dust and glory'

This is the great battle all men face. As long as we are on earth there is going to be a constant battle between the heavenly and earthly (Galatians 5.17), between what the Scriptures calls the flesh and the spirit. But the Bible also reveals that the Spirit of God helps man in his weaknesses (Romans 8.26) and we have a High Priest who lives forever to make intercession for us (Romans 8.34).

So Christian men should rejoice and take heart.

Though the battle for integrity is fierce, we are not alone.

We have the example of Jesus.

We have the help of the Holy Spirit.

And we have each other — the band of brothers.

BEHOLD THE MAN

PART 3:

THE CHRISTIAN MAN

BEHOLD THE MAN

PROLOGUE

Having looked at a Biblical view of manhood and masculinity, and then the Roman understanding of the manly man, we now come finally to a vital question: 'what should Christian men in the twenty first century aspire to embody when it comes to manly virtues?'

This question could be answered in many and diverse ways but in this final part of our book we have decided to stay true to some of the themes in Parts 1 and 2 and to look at just seven of the virtues that we believe the Christian man is called to cultivate.

Given that there is such a fierce battle over manhood and masculinity we have decided to stay with a military theme (so loved by Rome) and to address our question using the Apostle Paul's famous passage about the Armour of God.

This passage occurs in the Book of Ephesians, a letter whose authorship has traditionally been keenly contested. In this book, we take the view that *Ephesians* is a prison letter written by the Apostle Paul and that he dictated it while he was in chains, very probably seated between fully armed Roman legionaries — whose armour provided a very immediate visual aid for his exhortations.

It is in this setting that we imagine the courageous Apostle, who has himself fought the good fight, issuing a call to arms to the soldiers of Christ in the church of Ephesus, situated in the Roman province of Asia Minor.

Paul has already told his readers that they are seated in the heavenly places with Christ. He has also encouraged them to walk in a way that is worthy of their calling. Now, having told them to appreciate where they are seated and to take care how they walk, he gives them the order to stand.

Paul writes:

Finally, my brethren, be strong in the Lord and in the power of His might. Put on the whole armour of God that you may be able to stand against the wiles of the devil. For we do not wrestle against flesh and blood, but against principalities, against powers, against the rulers of the darkness of this age, against spiritual hosts of wickedness in the heavenly places. Therefore take up the whole armour of God, that you may be able to withstand in the evil day, and having done all, to stand. Stand therefore, having girded your waist with truth, having put on the breastplate of righteousness, and having shod your feet with the preparation of the gospel of peace; above all, taking the shield of faith with which you will be able to quench all the fiery darts of the wicked one. And take the helmet of salvation, and the sword of the Spirit, which is the word of God, praying always with all prayer and supplication in the Spirit, being watchful to this end with all perseverance and supplication for all the saints — and for me, that utterance may be given to me, that I may open my mouth boldly to make known the mystery of the gospel, for which I am an ambassador in chains; that in it I may speak boldly, as I ought to speak.

No one can avoid the sense of a 'call to arms' in these words. In fact, Professor Andrew Lincoln (author of one of the finest commentaries on the Letter to the Ephesians) has convincingly argued that Paul's rhetoric here has parallels with famous speeches made by Greek and Roman Generals to their armies in preparation for battle. This just confirms the fact that Paul chooses to end his magnificent letter with a stirring and impressive call to arms — a call to put on the armour of God and to make a stand against the forces of darkness intent on destroying the church and its faith.

In issuing this rousing call Paul enlists the imagery that is right before his weary and aging eyes — the armour worn by the Roman legionaries all around him in the jail where he is being held captive.

Paul orders his readers to wear the 'panoply' — in other words, 'the complete kit which a Roman soldier was expected to wear.' The historian Polybius gives a helpful description of this panoply. His list contains descriptions of the legionary's sword, two sorts of javelin (or spear), the brass helmet (and its striking plumes of feathers), and the breastplate. He also makes reference to a coat of chain-mail worn by some soldiers instead of the much heavier brass breastplate.

This is Polybius' description:

'The Roman panoply consists firstly of a shield (*scutum*), the convex surface of which measures two and a half feet in width and four feet in length, the thickness at the rim being a palm's breadth. It is made of two planks glued together, the outer surface being then covered first with canvas and then with calf-skin. Its upper and lower rims are strengthened by an iron edging which protects it from descending blows and from injury when rested on the ground. It also has an iron boss (*umbo*) fixed to it which turns aside the most formidable blows of stones, pikes, and heavy missiles in general.

Besides the shield they also carry a sword, hanging on the right thigh and called a Spanish sword. This is excellent for thrusting, and both of its edges cut effectually, as the blade is very strong and firm.

In addition they have two pila [spears], a brass helmet, and greaves. The *pila* are of two sorts — stout and fine. Of the stout ones some are round and a palm's length in diameter and others are a palm square.

Fine *pila*, which they carry in addition to the stout ones, are like moderate-sized hunting-spears, the length of the haft in all cases being about three cubits. Each is fitted with a barbed iron head of the same length as the haft. This they attach so securely to the haft, carrying the attachment halfway up the latter and fixing it with numerous rivets, that in action the iron will break sooner than become detached, although its thickness at the bottom where it comes in contact with the wood is a finger's breadth and a half; such great care do they take about attaching it firmly.

Finally they wear as an ornament a circle of feathers with three upright purple or black feathers about a cubit in height, the

119

addition of which on the head surmounting their other arms is to make every man look twice his real height, and to give him a fine appearance, such as will strike terror into the enemy.

The common soldiers wear in addition a breastplate of brass a span square, which they place in front of the heart and call the heart-protector (*pectorale*), this completing their accoutrements; but those who are rated above ten thousand drachmas wear instead of this a coat of chain-mail (*lorica*).

The *principes* and *triarii* are armed in the same manner except that instead of the *pila* the *triarii* carry long spears (*hastae*).'

Notice the similarities and the differences with Paul's description.

Polybius and Paul both make references to the shield, sword, helmet, and breastplate. However, Polybius includes items which Paul omits. He makes references to different kinds of spears. Paul omits these but mentions items that Polybius neglects: notably, the belt and the shoes.

The biggest difference of all between these two descriptions is however to do with the nature of this armour. Polybius is referring to physical realities — to literal, tangible armour pieces. Paul, on the other hand, is referring to spiritual realities — to moral and supernatural qualities. Indeed, Paul describes his panoply as 'the armour of God.'

This phrase could be taken in two senses. It could first of all mean 'the armour that God gives and which now belongs to us,' or secondly 'the armour worn by God himself which he permits us to use as well.'

If we exploit the first interpretation, then these pieces of armour are vital resources that God gives to his sons and daughters as gifts. If you want a picture from literature, think of the lion Aslan sending Father Christmas to give three of the children in Narnia their tools for the battle against the Witch's army — a sword and a shield, a bow and arrows and a dagger and a phial of healing oil.

If we accept the second interpretation, think of God Almighty as the Divine Warrior dressed in his own armour, as it says in the

Book of Isaiah:

He put on righteousness as a breastplate, and a helmet of salvation on His head; He put on the garments of vengeance for clothing, and was clad with zeal as a cloak.

[Isaiah 59.17]

Now imagine God giving you his own armour to wear – not like Saul's armour given to David (which didn't fit or suit him) but armour that is perfectly tailored to our Christian identity and destiny. Think of yourself wearing the armour pieces belonging to Yahweh the Warrior King.

If that doesn't call forth your redemptive manhood, we doubt whether anything will!

Paul tells his readers to wear this armour and to stand.

Notice his threefold call to stand in Ephesians 6.10-18.

Put on the whole armour of God that you may be able to stand against the wiles of the devil.

Therefore take up the whole armour of God, that you may be able to withstand in the evil day, and having done all, to stand.

Stand therefore, having girded your waist with truth, having put on the breastplate of righteousness, and having shod your feet with the preparation of the gospel of peace.

Three times in a short space of time, Paul uses the Greek verb *histemi*, to stand.

Sometimes a soldier's call is not to advance and take new ground but actually to make a stand on the ground already claimed.

That is what Paul is saying here. He has stated in the earlier chapters of his letter that Christ has already won the victory over the wicked forces that seek to disrupt the cosmos and divide the church. Christ rules above these principalities and powers and the adopted sons and daughters of God sit with him in this position of ultimate spiritual authority and sovereignty in the heavenly realms. The outcome of the battles which we fight are accordingly not in doubt. We do not fight for victory; we fight from victory. The call is not to advance — as if there is territory yet unconquered by Christ the Victor. It is to stand — to stand as an individual with resolute faith and determination, and to stand as a community — as the army of God — with the discipline and courage of a well organised and well trained Roman legion. Both individually and corporately we stand on the sure knowledge that Christ the King has conquered.

Who, then, is our enemy?

Although there is a plurality of demonic forces ranged against us, Paul maintains that there is a single malevolent intelligence behind these powers, orchestrating them for our destruction. As Andrew Lincoln puts it, in the worldview of Ephesians there is 'an ultimate personal power of evil behind these forces opposed to human well-being.' In Ephesians 2.2 he is called 'the ruler of the realm of the air' and in 4.27 he is referred to as 'the devil'.

This evil archenemy of God sets hostile entities against the church — entities which Paul mentions but does not define. He simply refers to them as principalities, powers, rulers and hosts of wickedness. All we know is that these forces are characterised by 'darkness'; they are not physical entities (i.e. 'flesh and blood'); and they operate 'in the heavenly realms' (in the spiritual realm beyond earth and beneath the throne of God where Christ is seated).

Christians are not to be afraid of these powers for two very good reasons.

First, the victory over these demonic forces has already been won through the death, resurrection and Ascension of Christ. Even though Paul amasses synonyms and gives the impression of gathering forces and increasing hostility in Ephesians 6.10ff, he is adamant that Christ has conquered our enemies and that they are fighting a losing — in fact, a 'lost' — battle. So even though there is great and intensifying darkness all around us (Ephesians 4.18; 5.8; 5.11; 6.12), the victory is certain. Like Frodo and Sam at the Battle of Helm's Deep, it is only a matter of time before the light appears in all its death-destroying radiance and the hordes of hell are crushed. All we are called to do is to stand with one another in unbreakable ranks of unity.

The second reason why we are not to fear is because our Heavenly Father has given us his dynamic and superior resources in the battle.

The primary resource we have is the Holy Spirit. Earlier in Ephesians, Paul has piled up words to do with the Spirit's strength in order to reassure believers that we are the recipients of indomitable power. In fact, he prays that we may all know in experience 'what is the exceeding greatness of His power toward us who believe, according to the working of His mighty power which He worked in Christ when He raised Him from the dead and seated Him at His right hand in the heavenly places' (Ephesians 1.19-20). What a glorious encouragement! The power that raised Christ from the dead is at work within us as we fight the good fight.

In Ephesians 6.10 Paul reinforces this truth by using three different words for 'strength'.

Finally, my brethren, be strong [endunamoo] in the Lord and in the power [kratos] of His might [ischus].

He also indicates that every member of the Trinity is involved in helping us to make our stand.

We are to wear the armour 'of God' (i.e. the Father's armour).

We are called to be strong in 'the Lord' (i.e. 'in Christ, who is Lord').

We are tasked to pray 'in the Spirit' (i.e. in the Holy Spirit).

So we should not give way to fear but rather stand with faith. The Father, the Son and the Holy Spirit are on our side and by our side. Christ has conquered and we share in his conclusive victory. The divine and grave-busting power of the Holy Spirit is working in us to make us more than overcomers.

Above all, we have the complete armour of our Warrior Father in heaven to help us.

We have the belt of truth.

We have the breastplate of righteousness.

We have the shoes of the gospel of peace.

We have the helmet of salvation.

We have the shield of faith.

We have the sword of the Spirit.

And we have prayer.

In this final phase of our book, we want to examine these weapons of spiritual warfare — inspired by the Roman soldier's panoply — and describe them as virtues which the Christian man is called to nurture in his life.

Christian men are strengthened in the spiritual battle as they clothe themselves in God's virtue. As Wycliffe's translation of Ephesians 6.10 reads, *here afterward, brethren, be ye comforted in the Lord, and in the might of his virtue*. Once we are dressed in God's virtue, we are strong indeed.

In *Behold the Man* we want to interpret every piece of armour as a symbol of the kind of virtue that Christian men are called to embody. Christian men are called to be truth tellers. We are called to live in a right relationship with God, to behave rightly and to promote the rights of those whose rights are ignored. We are called to be those who bring peace to those who are at war with God and with others. We are called to keep our minds focused on our true identity in Christ and to be steadfast in our convictions that Jesus Christ is Lord. We are called to be men who speak the word of God and people of Spirit-empowered prayer.

In saying all this, we do not want to imply that these seven virtues cannot be embraced by Christian women too. Although the imagery in Ephesians 6.10-20 is undeniably masculine in its original setting (only men could become Roman legionaries in Paul's day, after all), it would certainly not have been Paul's intention to imply that the armour of God can only be worn by Christian men. That would go against everything he has said earlier in Ephesians about the radical unity that is now available through the death of Christ

— a death which has destroyed the dividing walls which separate us, including the walls that divide men and women.

Having said that, we believe these seven pieces of armour can be used as an inspiration to Christian men to embrace a truly Christ-like image of manhood and masculinity. If those of us who are men were to accept this call, we have no doubt that this would mean liberation for women as well.

So our objective in this third and final part of Behold the Man is to take the seven qualities that Paul mentions — truth, righteousness, peace, salvation, faith, the Word and prayer — and see what they might say specifically to Christian men in the twenty first century.

In doing so we want to continue what we started in Part Two and highlight the differences between following Christ and following Caesar. Just because Paul uses the imagery of Roman armour doesn't mean that he accepts the methods of the Roman war machine. In fact, our view is that Paul is subverting the Roman way of enforcing peace. The Roman way involved subjecting the peoples of the earth to *Pax Romana* through the love of force. The Christian way involves serving the peoples of the earth with the peace of Christ using the force of love. In this respect, Christian men seek to operate counter-culturally, rejecting aggression and resorting to the more subversive, non-violent way of love.

Perhaps it would be helpful here to provide an example of this more radical way.

New Testament theologian Walter Wink has a fascinating interpretation of a well-known passage in the teaching of Jesus. We are referring here to Jesus' remarks about 'going the extra mile', contained within the Sermon on the Mount (Matthew 5.38-42):

"You have heard that it was said, 'An eye for an eye and a tooth for a tooth.' But I tell you not to resist an evil person. But whoever slaps you on your right cheek, turn the other to him also. If anyone wants to sue you and take away your tunic, let him have your cloak also. And whoever compels you to go one mile, go with him two. Give

*to him who asks you, and from him who wants to borrow from you
do not turn away.*

Walter Wink comments that this was the 'hardest word to utter
in a context of conflict because it can be so easily misunderstood
as spineless.' On the surface of it, Jesus seems to be encouraging
an attitude of passivity in the face of oppression. He seems to be
encouraging the men that are following him to allow others —
especially the Roman occupying soldiers — to treat them like
doormats.

However, Wink suggests that this is far from the case. Taking the
third of the commands — about going two miles instead of one —
he explains how Roman legionaries used to wear heavy backpacks.
These contained his spare clothes, food, cooking utensils, mess kit
and weighed about 30lbs. Consequently, legionaries would often
require local men to carry these packs. While the locals regarded
this as thoroughly degrading and an abuse of their rights, the
soldiers would see it as one of the rewards for being the occupying
force in power.

Roman officers accepted that their soldiers could do this but
also required that they should not take it too far so they restricted
the length to one mile. In Jerusalem and the surrounding territories,
their legionaries could order a Jewish man to carry their backpack
but it was restricted to this distance and no further.

In context, Jesus' command to go two miles instead of the one
is now seen as a thoroughly loaded and indeed subtle response
to oppression. It is not an aggressive or a violent response, to be
sure, but it is one that would have turned the tables on the Roman
legionary who ordered you to take his pack. By refusing to return
it after the statutory one mile, and bearing it for an extra mile,
you would have caused your oppressor to break the rules that his
commanders had decreed. In the process, a non-violent response
would have turned the tables and the victimizer would have become
the victim – the one shaming would have become the one shamed,
and all this without a sword being drawn or a shield being raised!

This is the kind of wisdom from heaven which Jesus gives to his followers. Far from encouraging men to become passive doormats, he inspires them to take the initiative and to engage in an active but non-aggressive response to their oppressors which brings shame upon their shameful tactics. This is the non-violent way of love, which is why Jesus follows this teaching with the command to 'love your enemies.' This love is not some unintelligent, acquiescent and timid submission to abuse. It is far more subtle than that. It is in reality an extraordinarily clever and profoundly effective means of loving resistance to tyranny and injustice. It involves seizing the initiative and employing the tactics of heaven rather than earth.

As a further explanation, Walter Wink quotes Dr Martin Luther King's sermon delivered at Dexter Avenue Baptist Church in Montgomery, Alabama in 1957. He wrote this address while incarcerated for the bus boycott. Dr King personified 'love' in this sermon and put his words on the lips of love. According to Dr King, Love says,

'We shall match your capacity to inflict suffering by our capacity to endure suffering. We shall meet your physical force with soul force. Do to us what you will, and we shall continue to love you. We cannot in all good conscience obey your unjust laws, because noncooperation with evil is as much a moral obligation as is cooperation with good. Throw us in jail, and we shall still love you. Bomb our homes and threaten our children, and we shall still love you. Send your hooded perpetrators of violence into our communities at the midnight hour and beat us and leave us half dead, and we shall still love you. But be ye assured that we will wear you down by our capacity to suffer. One day we shall win freedom, but not for ourselves. We shall so appeal to your heart and conscience that we shall win you in the process and our victory will be a double victory.'

This is precisely the kind of philosophy embodied in Jesus' much misunderstood teaching on 'going the extra mile.' It is the opposite of how human cultures operate. It is not an example of 'the myth of redemptive violence' — the worldly view that you can only redeem your situation of oppression by resorting to violence (a mindset illustrated in many popular stories and films). That is not the way of love. The way of love is non-violent but non-violent does not mean passive or foolish. It means enlisting an alternative, prophetic imagination and bringing the counter-culture of heaven into the abusive and unjust situations of earth. It means engaging in peaceful, positive resistance.

All this has huge implications for the way we understand and apply the armour of God passage in Ephesians 6. When Paul mentions armour items he is not exhorting men to take up physical, literal arms and to resort to violence. No, his way is the way of Christ and the way of Christ is the way opened up by the Gospel of peace. Far from encouraging militant aggression or military action, Paul is therefore rousing us to stand firm in support of the Good News that Christ brings peace between man and God, and between peoples and nations, and he does that through non-violent and extreme love – the love that cries out to a warring world from a blood-soaked Calvary.

That is indeed a more excellent way.

As we look at the armour pieces in Ephesians 6.10-20, our prayer is therefore that they will inspire Christian men — ourselves included — to rise up in their redeemed manhood and masculinity in order to be conformed to the image of Christ, the Heavenly Man, not to Caesar or the current versions of him in contemporary culture.

Chapter 1:

THE BELT OF TRUTH

Imagine for a moment that you are a young Jewish boy, say nine years old, running on the streets of Jerusalem around AD 30. You are playing with several other friends, laughing as you chase each other through the crowded alleyways and the bustling markets. Suddenly you and your friends stop still. You can hear the sound of jangling metal and crunching boots. You dash into the entrance of a shop and stare out towards the sound. As you do, you see scores of Roman legionaries marching in perfect ranks down the centre of the main street. They are led by a centurion with a gloriously plumed helmet seated on a caparisoned horse. For a moment, the spectacle takes your breath away.

The traders and buyers part like the Red Sea in front of the officer and his troops. You watch, wide eyed and open mouthed, as the legionaries march by, their bronze body armour clinking against their metal belt buckles, the nail studs on the soles of their feet marking out a perfect rhythm on the stone streets, their eyes fixed in a look of extreme concentration on the centurion in front of them.

Even though they are pagans, carrying the insignia of Caesar, you cannot help being overwhelmed by the impressive sights and sounds of these marching men.

Later you will fashion a small sword and a shield out of wood from your father's carpentry shop and play at being warring soldiers with your friends.

However much you hate them, you will never forget them.

Their armour will gleam in the darkest recesses of your memory for the rest of your life.

The distant bark of the officer's commands will often wake you in the middle of the night.

When the Apostle Paul thought about the ending to his magnificent letter to the Ephesians he was a prisoner of Rome. He was in chains in a damp and cold jail cell, guarded by Roman soldiers.

As he considered how he was to compose his final exhortation, the Holy Spirit drew his attention to the men next to him in their splendid armour.

'I know how to conclude this letter,' Paul mused. 'I'll issue a call to arms and encourage my flock to stand firm like spiritual legionaries.'

As he dwelt upon that God-breathed idea, he reflected on the armour pieces and began to see each item of the soldier's panoply as pictures of Christian virtues.

The first of the items he mentions is the belt and he refers to this as the belt of truth.

Stand therefore, having girded your waist with truth.

[Ephesians 6.14]

In the original text, Paul doesn't actually mention a belt. However, he does use the Greek verb *perizonnumi*, which means 'to fasten a belt', and the noun *osphus* which means 'the hips' or 'waist'. It seems then the Apostle has in mind the belt worn by the Roman legionary. He is referring to the belt to which the Roman soldier's sword and dagger were attached.

To get a true picture of this, we need to remember that the first item a Roman soldier would have put on in the morning was a white, short-sleeved tunic that extended to his knees. This was kept in place over his body not only by his breastplate but more importantly by his belt, which held everything together at the very centre of his body.

This is what Paul has in mind in Ephesians 6.14.

The belt worn by the Roman legionary in Paul's era was known as the *balteus* and was one of the main things that distinguished a soldier from a civilian. Usually this took the form of a single waist belt made with leather and decorated with embossed bronze plates. These belt plates were given intricate designs made out of niello, a black alloy of silver and sulphur. When a man wore a belt like this it was the surest sign that he was a soldier. Indeed, the Roman poet Juvenal referred to the legionaries as 'armed and belted men' (*Satires* 16.48).

The importance of the belt to the Roman legionary must not be underestimated. It was a symbol of his identity as a soldier. Take away his belt and you strip him of his identity. Indeed, just as in today's world a detective is divested of their identity when their police badge is taken from them, so in the Roman world of Paul's day a soldier was deprived of their identity when their belt was removed. If a soldier was dishonourably discharged, their belt was confiscated. If insurgents wanted to disorient soldiers in a crowd, they used daggers to slice the belts from their hips.

We should therefore take great care not to underestimate the significance of the belt in the panoply mentioned by Paul. Just because it seems relatively unimpressive compared to the other pieces doesn't mean for a moment that it is unimportant. The legionary's balteus was quite literally central to him and held everything in place.

Thus it is that Paul begins his listing of the armour pieces with the belt.

What did Paul have in mind when he mentioned this piece of the panoply?

The first thing to say is that he was referring to a spiritual and figurative reality.

As with all the pieces of armour the belt of truth is a heavenly not an earthly piece of equipment. Elsewhere in his letters Paul writes of the weapons that are available to the Christian in the fierce spiritual warfare to which he is exposed daily.

Of course we are human, but we don't fight like humans. The weapons we use in our fight are not made by humans. Rather, they are powerful weapons from God.

[2 Corinthians 10:3-4]

The belt of truth is accordingly part of God's heavenly armour. Yahweh, the Divine Warrior, gives us this piece of His holy armour to wear around our waists. So the first thing to note is this refers to a spiritual reality.

The second thing to note is that Paul is talking about the belt as a symbol of 'truth.' Paul has already used this word a number of times in Ephesians:

*And He Himself gave some to be apostles, some prophets, some evangelists, and some pastors and teachers, for the equipping of the saints for the work of ministry, for the edifying of the body of Christ, till we all come to the unity of the faith and of the knowledge of the Son of God, to a perfect man, to the measure of the stature of the fullness of Christ; that we should no longer be children, tossed to and fro and carried about with every wind of doctrine, by the trickery of men, in the cunning craftiness of deceitful plotting, but, speaking **the truth** in love, may grow up in all things into Him who is the head — Christ.*

[Ephesians 4.11-15]

*Therefore, putting away lying, "Let each one of you speak **truth** with his neighbour," for we are members of one another.*

[Ephesians 4:25]

*For you were once darkness, but now you are light in the Lord. Walk as children of light for the fruit of the Spirit is in all goodness, righteousness, **and truth**), finding out what is acceptable to the Lord.*

[Ephesians 5.8-10]

From these verses we can see that the word 'truth' has at least two meanings in Paul's mind.

The first way in which Paul seems to use 'truth' is in relation to our beliefs, specifically with reference to the truth of the Christian message. In Ephesians 4.11-15, Paul tells us that the Ascended Christ has given various ministries to the church (he mentions apostles, prophets, evangelists, pastors and teachers here) so that we may not remain as spiritual infants but grow up into fully mature sons and daughters of God. Mature sons and daughters are men and women who know the true truth of the Gospel and who will not accept any alternative doctrines to the ones provided by the Apostles. Mature sons and daughters are not like frail boats on a windy ocean, easily moved by every new gust of spiritual teaching doing the rounds. Rather, they are like strong galleys whose navigators fix their eyes on the bright morning star that is Jesus Christ, never wavering under the pressure of deception and never altering course under the sway of false teaching. Guided by the apostles, prophets, evangelists, pastors and teachers in the church, the adopted sons and daughters of God stay true to the truth.

When Paul commands his readers to put on the belt of truth, he is therefore calling them to contend for the faith. He is telling them to guard and protect the truth of the Gospel against all attempts to pollute or dilute it. He is telling them and indeed us that Christian truth is a matter of life and death, that Christian truth is eternal, that Christian truth is absolute.

We can therefore say something definitive at this point about the Christian 'manly man.' The Christian man in the twenty first century is not a relativist — he is not someone who regards every worldview as relatively true, including the Christian one. No, the Christian man today puts the belt of truth around his waist. He dresses himself with Biblical, Christian truth every day. He immerses himself in God's timeless Word which contains eternal and absolute truth and he makes this true truth central to everything in his life, like a belt that holds everything together. He is a champion of the truth of the Bible and the power of the Gospel to transform lives. He is a resolute defender of the Christian faith against all attempts to reduce and revise it, to make it more palatable to the natural mind and to the spirit of the age. Above all, when false doctrine or demonic deception is assaulting the walls of the church, he lovingly calls his brothers and sisters back to the truth brought to us by the Man from Heaven, Jesus Christ, and he diligently resets the intellectual and moral compass in people's souls to the true north that is Jesus Christ, who called himself not only the Way and the Life but the Truth.

The first virtue that the Christian man needs to embrace is accordingly a firm commitment to the truth found in the God-breathed Scriptures and supremely embodied by Jesus Christ, who is true truth in person. This truth is the coherent centre of his life, making sense of everything.

However, this is not the end of the matter because Paul also seems to use truth in a way that's not just about beliefs but also about behaviour. This should not surprise us. It has long been noticed that these two things cannot be separated in Paul's mind. The first three chapters of Ephesians are very much about right believing. They are doctrinal in content. The second three chapters are very much about right behaving. They are ethical in content. In Paul's thinking, right believing and right behaving are inextricably connected. Once you believe correctly you can behave correctly; your creed will always influence and determine your conduct.

In light of this we should not be surprised to see that Paul uses truth in a behavioural way in Ephesians. In the two other passages we quoted earlier, Paul talks about speaking truthfully in the church. In other words, he stresses the importance of honesty over lying. In the church, careless and dishonest talk costs us dearly. It divides brothers and sisters against one another and allows the devil a place in a community in which he is supposed to have no legal right of access. Given that it is our unity that keeps him out, we should be careful not to do anything that fosters division – especially telling lies about or to one another, which is in any event an infringement of the commandment not to bear false testimony against our neighbour. Telling the truth at all times must therefore be central to the Christian disciple's way of life. It must be a non-negotiable virtue at the very core of our being.

Once again this has radical implications for Christian men. Not only are we to be passionately concerned to protect and proclaim the truth of God's Word. We must be equally committed to telling the truth at all times — whether this refers to speaking truthfully in the church, at home, at work, in the business community, on the sports field and so on.

Christian men must accordingly be known for their integrity. We commend the truth value of what we believe by behaving with such integrity that we develop a reputation for being truth-tellers. In that way our truthfulness as men begins to point to the truthfulness of our message. Our integrity as people confirms the integrity of the Gospel.

Mark writes:

'When I was a very young Christian I was being mentored by an older man who told me something I have never forgotten. Forty years later it still inspires, challenges and sometimes convicts me. He said to me that there are three Testaments that other people read. There is the Old Testament, the New Testament and the You Testament. He said that most people read the You Testament first. In other words, before they ever open a Bible to read it they look at and read what kind of a person you are. If your lifestyle and your character are Christ-like, then they will start enquiring about the Christ who inspires you. As they read the You Testament, they'll read the New Testament and the Old Testament too.'

Maybe this is what Paul is trying to teach us when he says 'put on the belt of truth.' This not only refers to believing the truth of God's Word. It also means behaving in a truthful way — in a way that highlights your integrity and honesty. When we promote honesty, we promote the Gospel. When we give in to deception, we undermine the Gospel.

The Christian manly man is therefore a soldier who daily dresses himself with the belt of truth.

He makes a firm commitment to go on believing the truth of

God's Word, in spite of the increasing and intensifying deception all around him.

He makes an equally strong resolution to go on telling the truth in all situations, even in cultural contexts where lying is commonly justified.

Truthfulness is therefore our first line of defence against Satan.

And this truthfulness extends to the way we look at our own lives – to being real about our weaknesses and failures, not presenting a false mask of strength and success.

In Psalm 51.6 King David said, 'behold, you desire truth in the inward parts, and in the hidden part you will make me to know wisdom.' The Common English Bible translation says, 'you want truth in the most hidden places; you teach me wisdom in the most secret space.'

A true mark of manhood is the desire for truth in our innermost being, in the places no one sees, the hidden places of our heart, the deep places of our being.

John writes:

'I have often cried and prayed for hours that Christ's truth sanctifies every faculty of my being, that God keeps me in the place of the straight, the narrow and the contrite, that His truth leads me and guides me.'

The church would quickly be revived if every man among us made truth central in our lives and allowed true truth to hold everything together.

It is surely time to start dressing ourselves daily with the belt of truth.

Chapter 2:

THE BREASTPLATE OF RIGHTEOUSNESS

If you were an enemy of Rome standing in a field, watching a legion or a cohort of Roman soldiers advancing towards you in tight formation, one of the first things that you would have noticed was their body armour. Roman soldiers in the New Testament era usually fought wearing heavy chest plates. Some legionaries were equipped with very light armour. They were called *expeditii* and advanced in front of the legionaries with pila or light missiles, fighting skirmishes before the main body of troops crashed into the front ranks of their enemies. But most legionaries wore a cuirass or breastplate, an articulated piece of armour made up of iron hoops and plates and edged with bronze.

The breastplate worn by a Roman legionary weighed about 20lbs and was probably worn over a padded garment that had three functions — to stop the armour from grazing the skin, to absorb the blows when the armour was struck, and to hold the armour tightly in place. Once worn, the cuirass gave protection to the soldier's back, shoulders, chest and stomach. In particular, it afforded a robust covering for the legionary's heart. As Polybius put it, the legionary called his breastplate the *pectorale*, 'the heart protector.'

As the Apostle Paul makes his final exhortation to the Ephesian congregation, he proceeds with his description of the armour of God in Ephesians 6.10-20. He tells his readers,

Stand therefore, having girded your waist with truth, having put on the breastplate of righteousness.

Notice what the breastplate represents for Paul — it represents 'righteousness.' In the Apostle's call to arms, the Christian soldier is called to place 'righteousness' as a protector over his heart.

But what then is 'righteousness?' One of the finest explanations of the word 'righteousness' was provided by the great Bible teacher John Stott in his commentary on the Sermon on the Mount (Matthew 5-7). Stott explained that righteousness is understood in three ways in the Bible.

The first sense of the word is 'legal.' Think of a law court for a moment. As human beings, we are all in the dock, guilty of sin. We are not in the right in God's eyes. We are very much in the wrong and we are condemned to die. But God the perfect Judge decided to offer us a way out. He sent his one and only Son into the world, Jesus Christ. Jesus Christ lived a completely righteous life and He paid the penalty for our sins so that we could be right before God (Isaiah 53.11-12).

This legal sense of the word righteousness is extremely important in Scripture, especially in the writings of the Apostle Paul. In the Letter to the Romans, Paul makes it clear that none of us can get right with God through our own efforts. It is only by putting our faith and trust in the finished work of the Cross that we can be in the right before God. It is only by faith in Christ that we can stand in the docks and hear those magnificent words, 'not guilty.' Thanks to what Jesus has done, God can offer us a pardon through which we are declared to be in the right – right in his sight, not guilty in his holy presence.

This is what many have traditionally understood as 'justification.' Although there has been much debate and no little controversy surrounding this long held way of understanding justification, we believe it is still a valid and vital view.

We believe that Christian men are called to rejoice every day that they are in a right relationship with God because of what Jesus has done at Calvary.

We believe that Christian men are to protect their hearts with the beautiful certainty of their justification, celebrating daily that they are legally in the right before God.

Daily the Christian man is called to stand with the Apostle Paul and remember the magnificent words in Romans 8.31-34:

If God is for us, who can be against us? He who did not spare His own Son, but delivered Him up for us all, how shall He not with Him also freely give us all things? Who shall bring a charge against God's elect? It is God who justifies. Who is he who condemns? It is Christ who died, and furthermore is also risen, who is even at the right hand of God, who also makes intercession for us.

What would happen to Christian men all over the world if they were to awaken each dawn with a sure and heartfelt knowledge that God brings no charge against them?

What if every Christian man was to rise up each morning with an unshakable awareness of their right standing before God and their honoured position in Christ?

Such men could truly change the world because their manhood would rest upon Christ's righteousness not their own perfection (Isaiah 64.6).

This is so important in the spiritual battle because the devil can find all kinds of flaws in our righteousness, but he can find no flaw or blemish in the righteousness of Christ. Through his own righteousness, Christ disarmed principalities and powers and he made a public spectacle of them, triumphing over them on the Cross (Colossians 2:15). When Christian men place the breastplate of righteousness over their hearts, they make Christ's righteousness their heart protector and in the process present a terrifying reminder to the enemy of his humiliation. As this happens, the enemy has to flee.

The first connotation of 'righteousness' is accordingly legal. The Christian man, formerly condemned, is now justified. He has been given a pardon by God the Father and there is now no charge against him. He guards his heart with this wonderful truth because he knows that the heart is the wellspring of his life. It is the place where faith displaces fear and shame is trumped by significance. He knows that if the heart fails in battle, the battle is lost. So he wears Christ's righteousness as his heart protector and makes this doctrine the source of his constant reassurance. Day by day he keeps on believing in his heart that Jesus is alive and confessing with his mouth that Jesus is Lord (Romans 10.9). This in turn keeps his heart free from trouble and centred in God's peace (John 14.1). No man can afford to forget or ignore the breastplate of righteousness.

If the first connotation of the word righteousness is legal, the second — according to John Stott — is moral. Righteousness in a legal sense refers to our right standing before God. Righteousness in a moral sense refers to our right conduct, our godly behaviour.

There is no doubt that in Paul's mind righteousness is not only about right standing but also about right behaviour. In other words, righteousness is not just legal it is also ethical. More than that, it is not just ethical it is extremely practical.

For this reason, Paul deals in Ephesians with real life situations and gives guidance on how we should 'walk' in the contexts of everyday living.

Thus Paul emphasizes the importance of imitating the Father as his dear children. He calls us to live as sons and daughters whose thoughts, words and actions reflect the counter-cultural values of heaven.

Paul therefore deals with down-to-earth issues like how we should speak (5.2-4), the expression of our sexuality (5.5), our time management (5.15-16), our drinking habits (5.18-21), marital relationships (5.22-33), harmony in the home (6.1-4) and right conduct in the workplace (5-9).

This is moral righteousness. It is a practical holiness code for daily life. And it is challenging because many if not all of us will feel like we haven't lived up to such a high calling. Some of us may be living right now with a sense not of moral righteousness but an acute sense of moral failure. How are we ever to live such a holy life?

Perhaps this would be a helpful moment to remember King David.

David was a remarkable leader and yet he fell spectacularly. He fell because he allowed his strength to become his weakness. One of his strengths was the ability to create strategies that would bring victory in battle. When he saw and lusted after Bathsheba one day, he used this same strategic ability to fulfil his desires. He made plans to commit adultery with Bathsheba and to put her husband in a situation of certain death. He then used his position as King to orchestrate the fulfilment of his lust.

The truth eventually came out, as it always does, and David was utterly heart-broken.

He began to weep with godly sorrow and deep repentance.

He cried out, 'create in me a clean heart, O God, and renew a steadfast spirit within me' (Psalm 51.10).

Having experienced moral failure, David implored the Lord that he would create (*bara* in Hebrew, meaning 'to shape, fashion, form') a clean (*tahowr*, morally pure) heart.

He prayed for God to do a re-creative miracle.

What was David doing here?

If we use the language of Ephesians 6, he was taking up his battered breastplate of righteousness and placing it over his heart once again. The heart is the seat of all our emotions — including the debilitating feelings of shame, fear, unworthiness and failure. It is the governing centre of all our conduct. As David knew all too well, the heart is the place where all our decisions concerning God are made. It is the very core of our being.

David put the breastplate over his heart again.

In his heart, he looked to restore his right standing before God.

And he resolved to act rightly in his behaviour.

In spite of the fact that David had taken another man's wife and effectively killed her husband — a loyal servant of his called Uriah —

God heard David's cry.

More than that, God saw beyond this very dramatic fall to David's core and in the process declared what was really true about him.

He said that David was a man after his own heart – a man who would do all his will (Acts 13.22).

What an extraordinary statement that is!

David's failure did not define who he really was. His heart did, and his heart was passionately committed to God's heart, his will to doing God's will.

But did not David sin greatly?

Yes, but God did not allow this huge lapse of judgment to become the final word about David's life. God did not allow this shame to dictate his legacy or determine his destiny.

And here is something even more extraordinary. Jesus Christ, God's Son, would later be born in the line of David. Jesus Christ himself would be called 'Son of David.' If David had been defined by his failure, he would have been disqualified from such an honour. But because he repented, and his heart's default setting throughout his life was so in love with God, he was not disqualified from this honour. Truly God does not see as man sees but looks upon the heart.

All this is a great encouragement for us as Christian men.

When we lift the breastplate over our shoulders and fit it over our chests, we lock a heart-protector into place.

If we have failed, we can cry out from our hearts to God and receive his forgiveness and restoration. We can then make a stand once again with a renewed heart for the ethics of the Kingdom, defined not by our past but by our position.

If we have not failed like David, we can cry out to God from our hearts for his power to enable us to remain faithful in our marriages, families, relationships, workplaces, businesses, finances, churches, and so on.

All this is because our heavenly Father wants his children not only to embrace legal righteousness. He longs for us to desire moral righteousness too.

In this he helps us, by giving us the Holy Spirit – the Spirit of holiness – so that we do not fight the world, the flesh and the devil in our own strength alone but with the resources of heaven. With such resources at work within us we can cultivate snow white purity in our innermost being and live as righteous husbands, fathers, sons, friends, colleagues, workmates, brothers and men.

We can, in short, live lives that are conformed to the image of the man, Christ Jesus.

This brings us to the third connotation of 'righteousness' which is social. Social righteousness refers to doing the right thing for those whose human rights are being ignored or denied. It refers to more than just our individual standing before God (the legal sense) or our personal behaviour (the moral sense). Social righteousness breaks us out of the personal or private sphere into the public arena. Social righteousness means contending for the civil rights of others. It means working hard for the liberation of the oppressed. It means bringing Christ's Jubilee to those enslaved by demonic powers operating through wicked social systems and structures.

This now leads us back to the principalities and powers against which Christian men are to make their stand. What did Paul understand by these principalities and powers in Ephesians 6.10ff?

Once again we need to remind ourselves that Paul mentions these dark and evil realities without ever defining them. However, this does not mean that there is nothing we can say about them. Of particular significance is the social connotation of words like 'principalities' and 'rulers.' These suggest that Paul has in mind entities that affect the way that societies are governed. They point to demonic influences over entire cultures.

Walter Wink helpfully interprets these powers as 'seats of authority, hierarchical systems, ideological justifications, and punitive sanctions which their human incumbents exercise and which transcend these incumbents in both time and power.' They are not people, or 'flesh and blood.' They are demonic ways of thinking and operating which are employed by people to exploit other people. These invisible mind-influencers are superior to people because they operate 'in the heavenly realms.' They precede and transcend those who bow down to them and those who are disempowered and destroyed by them.

Describing these powers as heavenly realities is no license to become overly spiritual. Put another way, it is no excuse for becoming so heavenly minded that we are no longer any earthly use. Just because they operate in the heavenly realms doesn't provide a rationale for becoming careless or forgetful of the plight of those denied justice on the earth. In fact, Francis Shaeffer says it implies the exact opposite:

'The primary battle is a spiritual battle in the heavenlies. But this does not mean, therefore, that the battle we are in is otherworldly or outside of human history. It is a real spiritual battle, but it is equally a battle here on earth in our own country, or own communities, our places of work and our schools, and even in our own homes. The spiritual battle has its counterpart in the visible world, in the minds of men and women, and in every area of human culture. In the realm of space and time the heavenly battle is fought on the stage of human history.'

For the Christian man this has sobering implications. It means that we can no longer sit in our seats, in our pews, in our armchairs, passive and indifferent to the cries of the orphan and the widow. Rather it means that we have been commanded to take up and put on the armour of God, including the breastplate of social righteousness. We have been called to guard our hearts against a selfish, privatised spirituality and to allow the Father's love to ignite us with a compassion for the lost, the last and the least. We have been commanded to enter the battle grounds of this world — arenas such as government, media, the arts, education, family, economics, etc — and to promote practical action on behalf of the fatherless, the homeless, the destitute and so forth. Above all, we have been summoned to bring the culture of heaven to those who are experiencing hell on earth, ushering in the reign of the King of

Kings in the darkest places.

In the end, the Christian man gives his life for a purpose greater and higher than his own.

Just as *iustititia* (justice) was a cardinal virtue for the Roman manly man, so a passion for social justice is one of the virtues of a true man of God.

This longing for justice is a heart protector.

It is a heavy and effective breastplate in the battle.

It guards the heart against self-indulgence and sin and it keeps the heart close to the beating heart of Jesus, the archetypal manly man and the true champion of justice.

To summarise then, Christian men are called to put on the breastplate of righteousness.

This righteousness is first of all legal. Christian men are urged to remain in Christ and at peace with God.

It is secondly moral. In Christ, Christian men are called to think, talk and act in a righteous way in every context.

It is thirdly social. Christian men are tasked to stand up for the rights of those who are oppressed by flawed social systems – by what Paul calls principalities and powers.

This is a high calling indeed!

How is this to be achieved in practice?

Here we want to say a few words about the importance of men's accountability. Men are not supposed to attempt to live a legally, morally, socially righteous life on their own. We are called to live in community. In particular, we are wise if we submit ourselves out of reverence to Christ to a small group of other men who are committed to living holy lives. All of us need righteous brothers.

Perhaps once again Paul's picture of the Roman army can inspire us here.

When we look at the way a Roman legion was organized it is

fascinating to see how it was organized. Usually a legion comprised about 5400 men. These 5400 were divided into cohorts (480 men in each) and the cohorts into centuries (about one hundred men in each, as the term implies). Each century was in turn made up of ten smaller units of ten men — eight legionaries and two auxiliaries. This smallest unit was known as the *contubernium*, on account of the way this group of ten shared a tent together on campaigns.

The effectiveness of the Roman army had a great deal to do with its appreciation of the value and importance of the *contubernium*, the smallest unit. These men helped each other on with the heavier pieces of their armour — like the breastplate — and with their packs and other baggage. They also covered each others' backs in the battle, fighting as a group rather than isolated individuals. These men became friends and fought with and for each other.

Mark writes:

'One of the things I regret most, looking back over thirty plus years as a Christian, is my failure to believe in the importance of finding and joining a *contubermium* or a small band of brothers.

When I was at theological college I saw the value of such a small group of men. I was part of a prayer quartet with three other men – Gordon, Adrian and Hadge. When I was ordained and married, we all four went our separate ways and I stopped meeting with other Christian men for honest confession and mutual prayer.

Today, as I look at my life on the far side of failure, I wonder what might have happened (or not happened) had I created or joined a holy *contubernium* and not only covered other men's backs, but also had them covering mine. I know at least that having other men help me carry my heavy loads would have been immensely supportive. Having a group of fellow tent-dwellers would have enabled me to face my immense battles in a loving fraternal community rather than in isolation, which is what I chose instead. Maybe my flaws can be a lesson for others — that righteousness is most effectively lived when we have a small group of men who are committed to conforming their lives to the image of Christ and helping each other on with their breastplates.'

Chapter 3:

THE SHOES OF READINESS

In the Roman Empire of Paul's day you could tell that someone was a soldier by two items of their clothing. The first was their belt (*balteus*) — the decorated single waist belt we described in chapter 1. The second was their *caligae* or their strapped boots. If a man was walking in the street with a long sleeveless tunic tied by a military *balteus* you could be almost certain he was a legionary. If you looked at his footwear and saw that he was also sporting a pair of *caligae*, you could be absolutely certain.

What were these boots like? They were heavy-duty half-boots with iron-nailed soles. Their soles, in fact, were remarkably advanced. These nailing patterns gave support to the heel, arch and ball of the soldier's feet and allowed for considerable grip and manoeuvrability. In his book on the *Roman Legionary 58 BC — AD 69* (the source for some of our material on the Roman soldier's armour in these chapters), Ross Cowan says these heavy sandals were 'the precursors of the sole patterns on modern training shoes.'

Although there is some debate about when exactly these *caligae* became standard issue in the Roman army, we do know that by the time of the Emperor Augustus' reign these boots had become the regular footwear for Roman legionaries. Along with the jangle of the metal on their belts, it was the distinctive crunching sound of these iron-nailed shoes on stone streets and roads that would have indicated the imminence of Roman soldiers.

With that in mind, we return to Ephesians 6. When the Apostle

Paul told his readers to dress for spiritual warfare, the first item he mentions is the belt of truth and the second the breastplate of righteousness. Now he turns his attention to the Christian soldier's footwear.

Stand therefore, having girded your waist with truth, having put on the breastplate of righteousness, and having shod your feet with the preparation of the gospel of peace.

There is a lot to unpack in this third clause concerning footwear for the fight.

Notice that the word sandal, *hupodemata*, isn't used here but the verb *hupodeo* is. In the original Greek text Paul says 'having fitted your feet with the readiness of the gospel of peace.' Although he doesn't specifically mention them here, Paul was thinking of the *caligae* worn by the Roman legionary.

At the same time the emphasis on feet rather than actual footwear suggests that Paul also has an Old Testament quotation in mind. We are referring of course to Isaiah 52.7, 'how beautiful on the mountains are the feet of him who brings good news.'

This brings us to the words 'good news.' Paul says that we are to fit our feet with the readiness or preparation of the gospel of peace. The word 'gospel' means 'good news' and was used in the Roman Empire when heralds ran into cities in the Empire to announce good news about the Emperor.

'Good news! Good news!' they would shout. 'Our great Emperor has conquered our enemies.'

What then did Paul mean by the 'readiness' or 'preparation' of the gospel of peace?

Many people are inclined to look at this statement rather casually and assume it means 'being always ready to share the Gospel that brings peace.' However, Andrew Lincoln suggests that the real meaning is more complex; he claims it means 'the readiness that comes from the gospel of peace', not the readiness to proclaim the gospel of peace.

To understand this we must go back in the letter to Ephesians 2.14-18 where Paul announces that Christ is our peace. Christ has made peace both vertically and horizontally through his death on the Cross. In other words, he has reconciled men and women to God (the vertical dimension of peace-making), and has also reconciled men and women to each other (the horizontal dimension of peace-making). The greatest illustration of this in Paul's time was the fact that both Jews and Gentiles (who had formerly always been at enmity with each other) had been reconciled through the Cross and were now worshipping the Father through Jesus in the presence of the Holy Spirit. The dividing wall had come crashing down and what was deemed impossible — Jews and non-Jews loving each other — had become possible in the earliest Christian church.

In light of this, we can see how the Gospel of Jesus Christ truly is a Gospel peace. It is Good News which brings warring factions into an unexpected and welcome place of peacemaking and harmony. What human politics is always trying to achieve with limited results and over many years, Christ achieves with extraordinary results and over a very short space of time. He brings peace. *Pax Christiana* is far more powerful than *Pax Romana* could ever be.

At the same time, the new *shalom* or harmony has created an intensification in the spiritual warfare in our planet. The devil knows that the Cross means that he is already defeated. All his attempts to separate and divide people from God and each other are now exposed and disarmed at Calvary. They are furthermore confounded by the church. The church, now filled with people who love rather than hate each other, is a reminder not only of his past defeat at the Cross but also his future demise at the last judgment, where cosmic harmony will be established in and through Jesus Christ. No wonder the devil hates the church just as he hates Christ!

What this means is that the Gospel of peace has resulted in an increase in spiritual warfare. This is of course a paradox. The peace achieved through Christ's death, resurrection and ascension has resulted in the dark powers of the universe fighting even more ferociously. Even though Christ rules with supreme authority above these powers, and so indeed do we as his followers, these hostile entities still attempt to cause mayhem in the world and especially in the church, where their favourite tactic is to try to divide and conquer.

Think about it for a moment. Why is there division in the local and universal church? Surely if Christ has brought us a supernatural peace, there should be unusual harmony. Often times there is, but there are also times when the church becomes riddled with factions, or when churches rise up in pride and speak divisively of their superiority over other churches. Why does this happen?

Part of the answer lies in foolish choices made by those of us who all too fallibly follow Christ. But there is also a larger and more sinister reason. The truth is the devil wants to divide the church as much as possible because a united church defuses his powers but a fractured church gives him space in which to cause havoc.

This is why Paul tells the Christians in Ephesus to be very careful not to get angry with each other, to slander one another, to become bitter with one another. This kind of divisive behaviour, so often flowing from peoples' mouths, grieves the Holy Spirit and gives the devil a foothold in the church. Paul is deadly serious in Ephesians 4:25-28:

Therefore, putting away lying, "Let each one of you speak truth with his neighbour," for we are members of one another. Be angry, and do not sin: do not let the sun go down on your wrath, nor give place to the devil.

So here's what Paul meant by the 'readiness of the Gospel of peace': he means 'the state of maximum readiness for standing firm in the battle — a battle which has been intensified as a result of the gospel of Christ's peace being preached.'

Christians are therefore to be constantly ready to stand firm, wearing their *caligae* at all times in preparation for withstanding the onslaught of dark powers bent on the division and destruction of the church.

Every one of us in the church is to have our feet fitted with these spiritual army boots, and each one of us is called to make sure that our nail-studded soles are gripping hard into the ground won for us by Christ himself.

We are not to be found unprepared.

We are not to yield a metre to the enemy.

We are to stand firm and together, like holy legionaries, in ranks of unbreakable unity.

What then are the implications for the Christian man?

It is here that we must recognise the importance of the context of the armour of God passage. In the previous chapter of Ephesians, Paul has turned his attention to the issue of how Christians walk. This part of his letter begins in Ephesians 5.15-16 with the words,

See then that you walk circumspectly, not as fools but as wise, redeeming the time, because the days are evil.

In the verses that follow, Paul addresses a number of situations in which the Christian must intentionally resolve to walk in a holy, Christ-like way — in a way that befits the dearly loved children of a perfect Father.

The first context that Paul addresses is the home.

In Ephesians 5.22-30, Paul exhorts Christian wives to submit to their husbands and Christian husbands to lay down their lives for their wives. In Ephesians 6.1-4, Paul continues to apply his holiness code to the home by addressing children and their parents. Children are to obey their parents, in accordance with the Commandments, and fathers are to resist the temptation to exasperate their children.

From the home, Paul now moves to the workplace. In Ephesians 6.5-9, he urges Christian employees to be loyal and hardworking and Christian employers to be fair and kind.

Bondservants, be obedient to those who are your masters according to the flesh, with fear and trembling, in sincerity of heart, as to Christ; not with eyeservice, as men-pleasers, but as bondservants of Christ, doing the will of God from the heart, with good will doing service, as to the Lord, and not to men, knowing that whatever good anyone does, he will receive the same from the Lord, whether he is a slave or free. And you, masters, do the same things to them, giving up threatening, knowing that your own Master also is in heaven, and there is no partiality with Him.

Immediately after this passage, Paul moves on to describe the intensifying spiritual battle and issues his call to all Christians to wear the full armour of God. He begins this passage with the word 'finally,' indicating that his call to arms is the conclusion of his letter.

Now what is the importance of the placing of this call to arms directly after the exhortation to walk in counter-cultural holiness in the home and in the workplace? It is supremely important. For the Christian man it means being always ready at home and at work to make a stand against those demonic forces of destruction whose ire has been stoked by the preaching of the Gospel of peace.

This means that the true Christian man recognizes the divisive intentions of the dark powers of this universe and sees very clearly their strategy of fragmentation within the home and the workplace. He understands that the coming of Christ and the emergence of the church, the Bride of Christ, has resulted in these dark powers being defeated. But he also knows that defeated does not mean defunct and that these powers are still active – that in fact they are greatly increasing their activity in the war against Christ and his church. So the Christian man dresses as a soldier both at home and at work and achieves an attitude of maximum readiness to stand against the hostile forces that would divide wives from husbands, children from parents and employees from employers.

In actual practice, this shows that the Christian man is a man who will not allow his armour to be used against his wife, his children or his workmates. In the face of every temptation to turn his weapons against his own, he turns them directly and aggressively against the powers that seek to disrupt and destroy and he sends them packing with the heavenly weapons of the Divine Warrior himself. In the process, he sets an example to his wife and his children, encouraging them by his own example to turn their own weapons outwards towards the powers rather than inwards towards each other. And he sets an example in the workplace to all his workmates and indeed to his bosses of the importance of not allowing the enemy a foothold in the business. The Christian manly man always uses his armour against the enemy, not against his own kin or his own colleagues.

Sometimes, of course, this means that the Christian man must suffer. But in accepting this, the Christian man models the ministry of reconciliation contained within the Gospel — a peace-making ministry that is the furthest remove from the peace-enforcing tactics of the Roman Empire.

Here is Paul in Ephesians 2.14-18:

For He [Christ] Himself is our peace, who has made both one, and has broken down the middle wall of separation, having abolished in His flesh the enmity, that is, the law of commandments contained in ordinances, so as to create in Himself one new man from the two, thus making peace, and that He might reconcile them both to God in one body through the cross, thereby putting to death the enmity. And He came and preached peace to you who were afar off and to those who were near. For through Him we both have access by one Spirit to the Father.

Christ is the Prince of Peace and the Peacemaker. In fact, he is the personification and embodiment of Peace. He is the Shalom of Heaven – the one who reconciles the most warring tribes, nations and people through his death.

Yes, through his death.

It is through the suffering of his flesh upon a Roman Cross that Christ brings peace. It is through his shed blood that enmity is destroyed and peace is inaugurated.

This, then, has radical implications for Christian men. Paul has already urged Christian husbands to love their wives as Christ loved his bride the church. This means a lifestyle of self-sacrificial love. It means that there is a cost to be endured and a price to be paid, both within the home and in the workplace. Christian manly men are ready to suffer whatever it takes within the family and the workplace to get both family members and work colleagues to turn their armour outwards towards the powers rather than inwards towards each other. It means that Christian men are prepared to imitate Jesus and to suffer a moment in the flesh so that the already-won victory might be enjoyed forever.

And this ultimately is all about victory.

As the Christian man makes his stand, wearing his spiritual *caligae*, he knows that Christus Victor (Christ the Conqueror) has already won the decisive battle against these powers and principalities. He knows that even though the fury of these powers has been unleashed by this victory, that this demonic rage can be undermined and conquered by standing firm in the full armour of the Divine Warrior. He knows that Christ's victory can be applied in any and every situation through the use of heaven's ordinance.

So the Christian man is a man of victory.

Listen to the Apostle Paul's famous conclusion to Romans chapter 8 (verses 35-39):

Who shall separate us from the love of Christ? Shall trouble or hardship or persecution or famine or nakedness or danger or sword? As it is written:

"For your sake we face death all day long; we are considered as sheep to be slaughtered."

No, in all these things we are more than conquerors through him who loved us. For I am convinced that neither death nor life, neither angels nor demons, neither the present nor the future, nor any powers, neither height nor depth, nor anything else in all creation, will be able to separate us from the love of God that is in Christ Jesus our Lord.

Paul doesn't deny that Christians have to endure suffering. In fact, he lists seven types of suffering that we can expect: trouble, hardship, persecution, famine, nakedness, danger and even the sword. But he makes it clear that none of these has the power to separate us from the divine love and that in all of these things we can be victorious.

The word Paul uses here is the word 'conqueror'. This is in fact a verb in the Greek — *hupernikao*. It means to go beyond mere conquering! It means to be hyper-triumphant — 'super-achievers', to use today's terminology.

Notice the little word *nikao*. *Nikao* is a verb meaning to conquer and is used over twenty times in 1 John and Revelation alone. Nike is the noun form and it means victory or triumph. In the ancient world, Nike was a Greek winged goddess (Victoria in the Roman context) – an attendant of Zeus, the father of the gods, and a deity associated with speed, strength and triumph.

One of the best known athletic shoes in the world today is, of course, the *Nike* brand. Its logo is immediately recognizable from the high tech stadiums of America to the dusty football fields of Africa. The *Nike* brand is worth nearly 11 billion dollars and is the most valuable brand in sports businesses throughout the globe today. The tagline associated with the brand is, 'Just Do it!'

For the Christian manly man, the shoes of readiness are a critical piece of his kit for the spiritual battle. He has a pair of heaven's *caligae* at his disposal. These half-boots have extraordinary grip and are ideal for standing your ground when the terrain is rough and the winds are strong. On these shoes, heaven's brand is imprinted in the logo of a Cross — the symbol of Christ's comprehensive defeat of the powers and conquest over the devil. With these shoes, the Christian soldier is always prepared. He is ever-ready to respond with authority and efficacy to the demonic retaliation provoked by the proclamation throughout the streets of the world, 'good news! Good news! Our great Lord and Champion Jesus Christ has conquered all our enemies and peace has come.'

With these shoes, we can be more than conquerors.

We can encourage one another with the words, 'Just Do it!'

We can become manly men conformed to the image of Christ the Peacemaker, the Heavenly Man.

We can hear and receive the words of Paul in Romans 16.20, that 'the God of peace will soon crush Satan under your feet.'

BEHOLD THE MAN

Chapter 4:

THE SHIELD OF FAITH

Of all the items of the Roman soldier's armour it was the shield that was most essential for his protection. Polybius emphasized the importance of this piece of armour by listing and describing it first:

'The Roman panoply consists firstly of a shield (*scutum*), the convex surface of which measures two and a half feet in width and four feet in length, the thickness at the rim being a palm's breadth. It is made of two planks glued together, the outer surface being then covered first with canvas and then with calf-skin. Its upper and lower rims are strengthened by an iron edging which protects it from descending blows and from injury when rested on the ground. It also has an iron boss (*umbo*) fixed to it which turns aside the most formidable blows of stones, pikes, and heavy missiles in general.'

In the time of Caesar Augustus, the standard shield of the legionary was rectangular in shape. It was considerably lighter than its predecessor, weighing less than 13 lbs instead of the previous 22 lbs. It was only 5 mm thick and was held by its horizontal grip with a straight arm. It had iron edges and an iron, pointed boss in the centre. This was used with lethal effect as a ramming device when the front rank of a century of legionaries charged and punched violently into their opponents, shouting as they did. The boss would often cause the enemy to become unbalanced and fall over, whereupon they would be dispatched with the sword. In this light, we can see that the *scutum* was just as much an offensive as a defensive weapon, and that the all-too-often repeated line of the preachers — that the sword is the only offensive weapon in Paul's panoply — is incorrect. The shield was an offensive weapon as well.

On the outside of the shield, the wooden surface was covered by both canvas and the hides of animals adding an extra layer of protection. These were doused in water before every battle. Whenever the enemy applied pitch or tow to their arrows and ignited them, the soaked skins on the front of the legionaries' shields would not only absorb the blow, they would also extinguish the burning arrows. These burning arrows were known as *malleoli*.

It is quite obviously this picture that the Apostle Paul has in mind when he itemises the shield in the Christian's spiritual panoply. He does not list the shield first, as Polybius does, but he does tell his readers 'above all' (*en pasin*, which could also mean 'in all circumstances' or 'in addition to all these') to put on the shield. In Ephesians 6.14-16 he says,

> *Stand therefore, having girded your waist with truth, having put on the breastplate of righteousness, and having shod your feet with the preparation of the gospel of peace; above all, taking the shield of faith with which you will be able to quench all the fiery darts of the wicked one.*

Paul here likens our spiritual fight to a typical combat situation faced by a Roman legionary. He imagines the Christian church as a community of belted soldiers, with strong breastplates and nail-soled boots, raising their water-soaked shields to the fiery arrows sent against them. These malleoli are sent by the devil, described here as the 'evil one' (*poneros*). With this shield raised, either in front or above the soldier, the burning arrows of the enemy – not just some of them but all (*panta*) — can be countered and comprehensively neutralised. As Paul says, if Christian soldiers take up this shield, then they will be able (future tense) to protect their lives against every fiery assault sent by the wicked one.

All this is vital background for understanding the 'shield of faith.' While there is undoubtedly an Old Testament heritage for the shield image — not least the picture of the way Yahweh protects his people (see for example, Genesis 15.1; Psalm 5.2; 18.2, 30, 35) — there can be little doubt that the specific reference to raised shields and extinguished arrows comes from Paul's knowledge, as a Roman citizen, of the Roman war machine and its well-tested tactics. Paul is picturing his readers as spiritual legionaries standing in tight ranks, with their long rectangular shields raised in front or to the side (if they are in the front or on the outer edges of the formation) or above their heads (if they are in the centre). It is a graphic and rousing picture.

What then did Paul mean when he talked about this shield as 'the shield of faith? It may be a little contentious to bring the writer of 1 John into the discussion, given that we are examining one of Paul's letters, but the verses we quoted at the end of the last chapter when talking about the Christian's victory seem very relevant here.

In 1 John 5:4-5 we read,

For whatever is born of God overcomes the world. And this is the victory [nike] that has overcome the world — our faith. Who is he who overcomes the world, but he who believes that Jesus is the Son of God?

Here John talks about the importance of 'faith' for conquering what the world throws at us. This is the only time that the noun 'faith' (*pistis*) is used in the Gospel or letters of John so it is of note for that reason alone. But it is also important because it shows that Paul is not the only New Testament writer to link faith with victory. If we want to overcome the world, the flesh and the devil, we must be men and women of faith.

So what is this 'faith?'

At the most general level, faith is quite simply the God-given capacity to believe with confidence those things that are not seen by the natural eye. Put more succinctly, faith means believing what you cannot yet see. We cannot see Jesus at the moment. He is alive in his resurrection life but he is not visible to our eyes in the normal course of our Christian experience. But this doesn't mean that he isn't real — that he isn't the most real expression of reality in the entire universe. Jesus Christ is real, resurrected and reigning. Even though we cannot see him in all of his royal and heavenly majesty, we believe that he rules over all the powers of the cosmos and that one day he will return on the clouds with unparalleled splendour and that every eye will see him. As we wait for this momentous day, we believe that Jesus is God's One and Only Son and we proclaim that even though the world may be in a forlorn mess, Jesus Christ is still on the throne of God in the heavenly realms. So while faith is to believe what you cannot yet see, the reward of faith is eventually to see what we currently believe.

What all this highlights is that for New Testament writers like John and Paul, faith is Christocentric. Christian faith is faith in Christ, simple as that. The content of faith is inextricable from the person of Jesus Christ. As John says in the quotation above, the indispensable key for overcoming the evil intentions and onslaughts of a fallen world is to keep on 'believing that Jesus is the Son of God.' Here the tense is present continuous. We have to go on believing in Jesus' divine sonship, even and especially when this seems the hardest thing to do. When the Christian is assailed by demonic deception and false views about Jesus — views which seek to make him a mere mortal or just a great prophet or teacher — the true Christian fortifies his faith in Christ.

All this is perhaps a useful introduction to Paul's understanding of the 'shield of faith.' For Paul too, faith means faith in Jesus. Put another way, faith for Paul means maintaining the highest possible view of Jesus of Nazareth. It means cultivating a sustained confidence not only in his authentic divinity but also his unquestionable supremacy. To the man of true faith, Jesus Christ is regarded and revered as far greater, higher, stronger and wiser than every other expression of power in the cosmos. Faith means contending for a high Christology in a world where human beings in their sin-blinded ignorance and arrogance want to reduce Christ to just one of our kind rather than one of a kind. Faith for Paul means faith in the one who is seated in the heavenly places far above every principality, every title, everything.

Let's look at how Paul uses the word 'faith' in Ephesians in order to underline this point about its Christ-centeredness.

Here are some of the references:

I heard of your faith in the Lord Jesus

Ephesians 1:15

For by grace you have been saved through faith, and that not of yourselves; it is the gift of God, not of works, lest anyone should boast.

Ephesians 2.8-9

... that Christ may dwell in your hearts through faith

Ephesians 3.17

... till we all come to the unity of the faith and of the knowledge of the Son of God, to a perfect man, to the measure of the stature of the fullness of Christ

Ephesians 4:13

From these examples it is hard not to agree with the assertion that faith for Paul is inseparable from the person of Jesus Christ.

For Paul, faith is 'faith in the Lord Jesus.' Notice the word 'Lord.' This means more than just 'master.' In Latin the word is *dominus* and in Greek the word is *kurios*. To believe and proclaim that Jesus is Lord is to believe and proclaim that he is the ruling authority above every other ruling authority — including Caesar, who was also known as 'lord.'

For Paul, faith is what saves a person — saves them from a shameful and sin-centred life with all its destructive and disastrous consequences, saves them to a Christ-centred life with all its outrageous rewards, such as the matchless honour of being seated with Christ above the powers of this present age — a position which is to be enjoyed now.

For Paul, faith is what enables a person to have more than just an intellectual assent to truth. Faith is what enables a person to enjoy the indescribable privilege of having Jesus — the Lord of the Universe – dwelling in our hearts. By faith, Jesus Christ the Risen

King takes up residence in the core of our being and rules with love over our lives.

For Paul, faith is faith in Jesus as the Son of God. In his eyes, the Christian is a man or a woman who is wholly committed to spiritual maturity, growing into someone who truly believes that Jesus is God's One and Only Son, one who truly *knows* that Jesus is God's Son – not just cognitively but also affectionately.

When Paul tells us to take up the shield of faith, he is therefore not speaking about believing in anything. For him, there is a specific content to this faith. It is faith in Jesus Christ, a faith that inevitably brings the Christian into conflict with demonic powers.

There is a deep irony here because Paul has not only a piece of Roman armour in mind. He also has a Roman enemy in mind as well. In his eyes, the Christian is to raise his shield and that shield is likened to the Roman soldier's *scutum*. Yet in Paul's day one of the most terrifying sources of persecution were the very people from whom Paul plunders this weapon — namely, the Roman Empire! This does not mean of course that Paul was encouraging his readers to see individual Roman citizens as the enemy. Before he even mentions the armour of God in Ephesians 6.14 he makes it clear that our fight is not against flesh and blood (i.e. human beings) but against the powers that influence people. These powers use individuals – especially those in governmental influence – to place nations in bondage to worldly ideologies and fallen social systems. Paul's words may therefore be ironic – exhorting his readers to use Roman weapons against the attacks of the Roman Empire – but he is not advocating that his readers should hate or fight people but rather combat the powers that influence them.

All this is shown in even sharper relief when we look at how faith in Christ brought people into intense conflict with the dark powers that influenced the Roman Empire. For the Christian in the first century, raising the shield of faith meant lifting Jesus up in worship. To do this was not a comfortable thing at all – not like it is for so many in the consumer-driven Western world of today. To exalt Jesus in Paul's day meant hardship, trouble, persecution and even death. To proclaim Jesus as greater than Caesar could ultimately lead you to a martyr's death.

With that in mind, let's look at the content of the faith that Paul calls us to raise as a shield.

For Paul, faith in Christ meant believing, confessing and proclaiming the following:

1. JESUS IS THE SON OF GOD

In the Roman world, the Emperor was regarded as 'son of god.' Some of the Emperors after Caesar Augustus even believed this about themselves. In the language of the Roman Empire – which was of course Latin – the exact words were '*divi filius.*' Notice that the word used is '*divus*' not '*deus.*' *Deus* in Latin could only refer to the gods, in other words to deities. *Divus* had no such necessary connotation.

This kind of distinction was all well and good in a Latin-speaking context. Outside of those contexts, however, the main language spoken in the Empire was a form of colloquial (rather than Classical) Greek and in that language there was no such fine distinction between *divus* and *deus.* The Greek-speakers only had one word where the Latin-speakers had two. In Greek the one word is *theos.*

In Greek-speaking contexts, such as the world of the New Testament (which is written entirely in Greek), this presented a major challenge. To speak of the Emperor using *theos* could only mean one thing. Since *theos* was reserved for the Divine Creator, to call the Emperor 'son of god' — *huois tou theou* in Greek — meant ascribing divinity to him and to do that was blasphemous.

For a Christian in the Roman Empire of Paul's day, raising the shield of faith therefore meant something extremely dangerous. It meant promoting a conviction that Jesus is worthy of the honorific title 'son of God'. It meant contending against the dark powers which had fuelled the worldwide Imperial Cult and which had increasingly invested the Emperor with titles suggestive of divinity. In short, it meant wrestling against the deceptive and seductive ideology that inspired spiritually blinded and compliant citizens to believe that Caesar is Lord but Christ is not.

All this shows how important it is not to undermine or ignore the radical nature of faith in Christ in Paul's day. For example, when the Roman centurion at the foot of the Cross declares that Jesus is truly the son of God (Mark 15.3) we may be guilty of underestimating the significance of this confession. The Roman centurion would have known all too well that 'son of God' was a title reserved for his Emperor. Yet, seeing the extraordinary fortitude of the dying Rabbi in front of him, faith rises up in the man and out of his mouth comes a pronouncement that represents a surprising and potent challenge to the dark powers influencing the Imperial Cult. He says that Jesus, the crucified Nazarene, deserves the title 'son of God.' That was radical. Life for him from here on, if he continued to trust in Christ and remain in the Roman army, would not have been easy.

2. JESUS IS LORD

For Paul, faith in Christ meant believing, confessing and proclaiming not only that Jesus Christ is the Son of God but also 'Lord.'

Reading the start of 1 Corinthians 12, we may wonder why it is that Paul says that it is only possible to confess that Jesus is Lord except with the help of the Holy Spirit.

As Paul prepares to launch into a paragraph about the gifts of the Holy Spirit, he says this:

Now concerning spiritual gifts, brethren, I do not want you to be ignorant: You know that you were Gentiles, carried away to these dumb idols, however you were led. Therefore I make known to you that no one speaking by the Spirit of God calls Jesus accursed, and no one can say that Jesus is Lord except by the Holy Spirit.

[1 Corinthians 12.1-3]

'No one can say Jesus is Lord except by the Holy Spirit.' Surely it is a relatively easy thing to open one's mouth and say the words, 'Jesus is Lord!' Yes, maybe so, at least in the comfortable social context which many Western churches find themselves in the twenty first century. But this was not so in the first century where confessing that Jesus is Lord was an extraordinarily dangerous thing to say – something that could cost you your life. Only someone filled with the empowering and Christ-glorifying Spirit of God could say in that context something as courageous as this. Such a confession could never have been the product of natural resolve. It would have to be supernaturally inspired and motivated.

When a person became a Christian in the Roman Empire of Paul's day they did so because something momentous had happened in their hearts. They had come to believe with absolute certainty that Jesus of Nazareth, crucified on a Roman Cross, had not only died for their sins but been raised from the dead. This heart-felt conviction then produced a vocal declaration. People who owned the fact that Jesus was alive forevermore realised that he was 'Lord' in a way that a mortal Emperor could never be. They accordingly declared with their mouths that Jesus Christ is 'Lord'. This is why Paul says in Romans 10.9:

'If you confess with your mouth the Lord Jesus and believe in your heart that God has raised Him from the dead, you will be saved.'

In the New International Version this is even clearer:

'If you confess with your mouth, "Jesus is Lord," and believe in your heart that God raised him from the dead, you will be saved.'

Believing in the resurrection of Jesus therefore released a powerful confession in his Lordship. 'He's alive' led inexorably to 'he is Lord!'

In a world where Caesar was regarded and confessed as *dominus* (Latin) and *kurios* (Greek), this was extremely bold. Perhaps this is why Paul talks about the shield of faith in Ephesians 6.10-20. He knows that raising the shield of faith meant believing and confessing that Jesus Christ is Lord. He also knows that this meant confronting and engaging the dark powers that influenced millions of Roman citizens to confess that Caesar was 'lord'. Declaring Christ's Lordship therefore meant taking the shield of faith and ramming it into the ranks of the enemy, as it were. It meant counter-cultural courage – the kind of courage which arises from the emboldening fire of the Holy Spirit in a person's heart.

3. JESUS IS OUR PEACE

The Christian soldier is someone firmly convinced that Jesus Christ is our Peace. He is the one whose death on the Cross has brought about reconciliation both vertically and horizontally. Vertically, Christ's death has brought an end to the hostility between man and God — a hostility arising solely out of man's sinfulness and rebellion — and produced a lasting peace, a shalom in which man can now know God as his friend. Horizontally, Christ's death has resulted in the possibility of warring tribes and nations finding peace with each other. At the foot of the Cross, enemies become friends. Jews and Gentiles, at war with each other for many centuries, can now find access to the same heavenly Father as they enter into a living relationship with Christ through the power of the Holy Spirit (Ephesians 2.18). Men and women who have been at each other's throats can now know God as Abba, Father and – as his adopted, royal sons and daughters – become equal brothers and sisters in the family of God.

This is 'Gospel!' It is Good News! Christ, the Prince of Peace, has made peace and given us the ministry of reconciliation. He has given us the opportunity and the resources to proclaim the Gospel of peace and to lead people whom the politicians could never unite into a harmony that astounds the world and confounds the devil. This peace spreads throughout the world through the message of the Gospel, accompanied by miracles and acts of mercy.

This call to proclaim that Christ is our peace required courageous faith in the first century. To use the words of Ephesians 6, it required the Christian disciple to raise the shield of faith. Preaching this message was at the very heart of Christian mission and resulted in the missionary confronting the dark powers that motivated Roman citizens to declare that Caesar alone was the bringer of peace. This involved intense spiritual warfare.

Remember that in the Roman Empire, the word gospel (*evangelion* in Greek) meant 'glad tidings.' It was a word used of good news concerning the Emperor. On an inscription in Priene, dating from 9BC, we find these words about the Emperor Augustus' birthday: 'the birthday of the god was the beginning of the glad tidings of joy on account of him.' For the Roman man, Augustus' birthday was worth celebrating as 'good news' because the Emperor had brought peace to the world.

Yet the methods used by Caesar were altogether different from the methods advocated by Christ. In Caesar's case, peace was established by brute force. It was not the result of negotiation but of occupation. It arose out of destruction not out of diplomacy. The Roman historian Tacitus quotes some words of the British chieftain called Calgacus which highlight this cruel and oppressive methodology. Commenting on the Roman way, Calgacus comments that 'where they made destitution, they call it peace.'

Perhaps nothing demonstrated the paradox of bringing peace through war more graphically than the altar of peace in Rome. This ironically stood on Mars Hill (Mars being the Roman god of war). Roman citizens were quite content with this paradox.

How different this is from the way of Christ. Christ brought peace not by utilizing the victimizing forces of the Roman Empire but by submitting to them in loving, subversive and peaceful resistance at the Cross. As Paul says in Colossians 1.19-22:

It pleased the Father that in Him all the fullness should dwell, and by Him to reconcile all things to Himself, by Him, whether things on earth or things in heaven, having made peace through the blood of His cross. And you, who once were alienated and enemies in your mind by wicked works, yet now He has reconciled in the body of His flesh through death.

Colossians 1:19-22

Jesus Christ is truly the Peace Bringer. No wonder, when Christ was born, the angels announced that he was the Saviour and that he was bringing peace on earth. From a political view this was a direct confrontation to the good news that Caesar has brought peace to the earth through violence. Far from being a safe and quaint event, the nativity was accordingly a declaration of war. There was truly danger in the manger!

4. JESUS IS THE SAVIOUR OF THE WORLD

Another aspect of faith in Christ involved believing and proclaiming that Jesus is 'Saviour.' This was at the very heart of Jesus' name and it was at the very heart of his purpose. Jesus came to save people from their sins. Even the non-Jewish inhabitants of Sychar understood this. After encountering Jesus at the well they declared that he was 'the Saviour of the world' (John 4.42).

Again, such a confession required God-given and courageous faith. Confessing that Jesus the Jew was the global Saviour was no trivial thing, especially in the Roman Empire. The Roman Emperor was called 'Saviour' and indeed 'Saviour of the world.' By bringing order and peace to a chaotic and unruly planet, the Emperor was regarded and revered as the world's rescuer, deliverer and saviour.

This ability to bring peace to the earth was understood by Roman citizens over time as an attribute of divinity. Surely only a god or a demi-god had the power and authority to achieve such a colossal task. Surely only a deity could bring about a new world order where before there had only been warring barbarians and ignorant tribes. No wonder the cult of the Emperor developed into a full blown religion.

In the Roman Empire of Paul's day, there were two forces that kept the conquered world in a state of enforced peace. The first was of course the Roman legions. The second was the growing Imperial Cult, a cult which vanquished territories were quickly compelled to adopt. In this cult, people began to be seduced by the deception that Caesar was Lord of the world. Conquered peoples everywhere began to call him Saviour.

This deception was of course a political masterstroke. If occupied peoples could be persuaded to acknowledge Caesar as Saviour and Lord, then there would be far less need to keep them in line through the use of the expensive Roman war machine. All that was needed was blind devotion to the Emperor. It was therefore not just taxes that were given by defeated enemies. Sacrifices were expected as well.

It was in this context that the first Christians found themselves. They came to acknowledge that Jesus is the Saviour of the World and in making this declaration they immediately ran into conflict.

Faith in Christ meant faith in Jesus as the world's Saviour.

Faith in Christ as the Saviour of the world brought them into intense spiritual conflict with the prevailing dark powers in their world, which were Roman imperialistic powers.

Faith in Christ therefore required immense courage.

Standing for Jesus in a world of Emperor worship meant raising a faith-shield to the apotheosizing and deifying forces which had inspired and now sustained the Imperial Cult.

No wonder Paul said 'above all, take up the shield of faith.'

5. JESUS IS THE COMING KING

It is impossible to leave this topic without mentioning that faith in Christ has a future tense. It is not just a matter of believing certain things to be true in the past (that, for example, Jesus Christ was raised from the dead and thereby vindicated as the Son of God). Nor is it merely a matter of continuing to believe in the present that Jesus of Nazareth is the only human being in history who is also divine, and therefore worthy of titles like Saviour and Lord. It is also a matter of looking ahead to the future and trusting with a God-given certainty that Jesus Christ will one day come back to the planet that he visited and that when he does he will be acknowledged for who he really is – the King of Kings and the Lord of lords (i.e. the Lord who is far above others who are called 'lord', including Caesar).

Faith accordingly has an eschatological focus. It looks forward to the *eschata* — the last things of history. It gazes ahead to the future events prophesied in the Bible, including — citing Tolkien's terminology — 'the Return of the King.' In other words, faith in Christ means faith in the Second Coming of Jesus Christ on the last day of history.

Here we must give attention to one of Paul's most creative terms for the Second Coming of Christ, namely the word *parousia*, a Greek word that can be translated as 'appearing', 'arrival', 'advent', 'presence', or 'coming.' Perhaps the most detailed description of how Paul saw this *parousia* is in 1 Thessalonians 4:13-18:

*I do not want you to be ignorant, brethren, concerning those who have fallen asleep, lest you sorrow as others who have no hope. For if we believe that Jesus died and rose again, even so God will bring with Him those who sleep in Jesus. For this we say to you by the word of the Lord, that we who are alive and remain until **the coming of the Lord** will by no means precede those who are asleep. For the Lord Himself will descend from heaven with a shout, with the voice of an archangel, and with the trumpet of God. And the dead in Christ will rise first. Then we who are alive and remain shall be caught up together with them in the clouds to meet the Lord in the air. And thus we shall always be with the Lord. Therefore comfort one another with these words.*

Notice the words underlined 'the coming of the Lord.' The word translated 'coming' in the New King James Version is *parousia* in Greek (*adventus* in Latin). Paul uses this word four times in 1 Thessalonians and always and only with reference to the 'Lord Jesus.' For Paul, the final, climactic act of history is the *parousia* of Jesus Christ who is Lord.

Why is this so significant? The answer is because the word *parousia* was used in Paul's day of the arrival of the Emperor on a visit to one of his colonies or provinces. Before this happened, roads were repaired so that the Emperor could travel comfortably. Crowds assembled to pay homage as processions of white-clothed men and women marched ahead of the Emperor to the sound of many trumpets. In some cities even 'advent coins' were minted for the occasion.

In plundering this term, Paul brilliantly exploits the idea of an

Imperial visit by applying it to Jesus Christ. The future return of Jesus Christ on this earth is far more dramatic and significant than any sudden appearance of the Emperor in a Roman colony. It is Christ who is the true Lord of the world not Caesar. As soon as Christ the Lord returns, all things will be gathered together in one in the person of Jesus Christ — things in heaven as well as earth (Ephesians 1:10). The *parousia* of Christ will therefore mark the final end of all hostilities in both the heavenly realms and on earth and will accordingly inaugurate an everlasting shalom.

This future fact must have inspired first century Christians with an indomitable hope. In the midst of Roman persecution, they could look at the powers behind their oppression and say with Paul, 'one day there is going to be a *parousia* that will put an end to all this — a *parousia* that will far outshine anything that the Emperors have produced. When that happens, every demonic power will be annihilated forever and every social manifestation of those powers will be brought down, never to rise again.'

No wonder Paul could say to his readers in 1 Thessalonians 4, 'comfort one another with these words.'

When Christians in the first century raised the shield of faith, they fortified themselves with the inspiring truth that Jesus Christ is the true Lord of the universe and he is one day going to make a *parousia* which will terminate the persecuting powers – permanently.

Faith in Christ therefore has a future orientation.

It leads the Christian away from saying, 'look what the world is coming to,' and draws them instead to the place of faith – the place where they can say with confidence, 'look who's coming to the world.'

In summary, when Paul told his readers to lift the shield of faith he was telling them to raise their faith in Christ who is truly the Son of God, Lord, Peacemaker, Saviour of the World and Coming King — and many other things besides. Paul knew, as the Apostle John did, that this kind of Christocentric faith leads to the Christian walking in the victory won by Christ over the dark powers. This kind of faith leads to us being more than conquerors in the intense spiritual warfare triggered by the ever-expanding proclamation of the Gospel of peace.

And this warfare is intense. The wicked one is constantly firing salvos of flaming arrows at us — arrows of persecution, temptation, deception, oppression, victimization, marginalization and so on. These arrows are designed to immobilise us and render us inactive and unproductive in the spiritual battle. But we can counter them. God's armour is upon us and this armour includes an extremely effective shield with which these arrows can immediately be extinguished if we stand together in community.

For the Christian man who wants to be a manly man conformed to the image of Christ, this has huge ramifications.

Christian men today find themselves cowering under a dark cloud of cambering arrows. Under such an onslaught, it would be easy to give way to the seductions of the enemy and compromise in the area of beliefs and behaviour. But standing together in ranks – as opposed to vulnerable isolation – men of faith can raise their shields and say no to false teaching when it infiltrates the church, no to the temptation to conform to the world rather than stay true to the Gospel, no to the totalizing tendencies embodied by those who want a new world order, and no to the direct attacks of those whose anti-Christian aggression is motivated by the principalities and powers.

In Paul's day, the first Christians lived in a culture where the Caesars were deified. Some of them were spoken about in the most exalted terms. Caesar Augustus, for example, was called 'the Emperor Caesar, son of god, Augustus, ruler of all land and sea.' His rule extended from Rome, through the provinces, to the borders of the Empire. In these territories, a new world order characterized by pax Romana was established and those who stood against it were violently opposed and oppressed.

Today it seems that there is more and more talk of a new world order and more and more images of Empire around us. Indeed, some are even warning about the re-emergence of the Roman Empire in a rebooted form in our own times.

In such a context, Christian men are going to be called to make a stand for true faith in Christ, especially as the spirit of anti-Christ increases its activity in hostile, secularised social structures.

Men of God will need to make their stand in such a context and do so together.

Men of faith will need to call out to each other, 'shields up!'

They will need to be men who resolutely defend the doctrine of the divinity and the lordship of Christ.

They will need to be men of mission who humbly bring the Gospel of peace into their spheres of influence, demonstrating by their own servant hearts that *Pax Christiana* is far more functional, healthy and lasting than any expression of *Pax Romana* could ever be.

They will need to be men like the two Apostles, Peter and John, who declared that there is only one name by which human beings can be saved – the name of Jesus.

And they will need to be men who look forward with extreme eagerness to the Return of the King, when the spiritual war will finally end and the shalom of the Father will permeate every glory-filled particle of the new heavens and the new earth.

All this, of course, sounds heroic — epic even.

Who among us is worthy of such a calling?

Many of us have failed — some of us in little ways, others of us in dramatic ways.

It would be all too easy for many men, dismayed by a sense of personal failure, to disqualify themselves from the fight because of shame.

But here we must remember the beautiful and scandalous grace of God.

The truth is that God is much kinder to us than we are to

ourselves as men.

We need to keep our minds focused on the glorious truth that our redemptive Father believes in 'messiology' – turning our mess into a message.

We need to remember the many stories in which men who have fallen have been given another chance and sometimes a further chance beyond that.

Perhaps this is a helpful place to end.

One of the most glaring failures in Scripture, at least to preachers over the centuries, is so-called Doubting Thomas.

Thomas did not raise the shield of faith at a critical moment in his discipleship. He did not believe what his brothers believed — that Jesus of Nazareth had been raised from the dead and had appeared among them.

Thomas of course had been absent when the Risen Lord had appeared to the others.

Eight days later Jesus made another appearance, this time when Thomas was in the room.

Even though there were others there, Jesus appeared supremely for Thomas.

He organised a resurrection appearance for just one man.

When Thomas touched the wounds of Jesus and realised that it was indeed his friend and master, he declared, 'my Lord and my God!' (John 20.28).

Preachers have been far too quick to label Thomas as a doubter and in the process focus on his weaknesses rather than his strengths, his failure rather than his recovery. But that is both unfair and unwise. Thomas encountered the Risen Jesus and when he did he made a confession that was both courageous and revelatory. He pronounced in front of the brothers that Jesus was 'my Lord and my God!'

Do we have any idea how bold and radical that was? In the

Roman Empire in which Thomas lived, Roman citizens said of their Emperor that he was both *divus* and *dominus* (sometimes even deus et *dominus*). When Thomas feels the wounds of his Messiah, he uses exactly this language and calls Jesus his Lord and his God. No one in the fourth gospel gets close to saying anything as profound or as dangerous as this about Jesus Christ.

So don't be hard on Thomas and don't be hard on yourself.

Thomas came back from doubt to raise the shield of faith with exemplary boldness.

Thomas came back from failure to proclaim that Jesus — and not Caesar — was worthy of the titles 'Lord' and 'God.'

It took an encounter with Jesus to turn doubting Thomas into confessing Thomas.

That is what it takes for us too.

Failure need not disqualify us.

If we open up our hearts to the Risen One, we will encounter him too, and in that shame-destroying encounter find that our broken hearts are renewed, our broken ranks restored, and our broken shields repaired.

Isn't it time that Christian men raised the shield of faith again?

BEHOLD THE MAN

Chapter 5:

THE HELMET OF SALVATION

The helmet was an indispensable piece of armour for the Roman legionary. It was made of bronze and was essentially an oval bowl weighing 4-5 lbs with a rear peak which jutted out at the nape of the neck. This was designed with small ridges or steps which acted to break the force of downward blows, deflecting them onto the neck guards. At the sides of the helmet there were metal flanges or cheek guards to protect the face and throat. These hung down to the neck line and had holes for the ears to allow the legionary to hear orders in battle. These cheek pieces, along with the oval bowl of the helmet itself, were lined with woollen felt to absorb blows and increase comfort. All in all, the legionary's helmet was a superbly designed item of armour.

After urging his readers to put on the belt, breastplate, the shoes and shield, Paul now tells them to 'take up' the helmet. 'Take up' is the New King James Version but the verb should be translated 'receive.' After the participles in verses 14-16 ('having girded', 'having put on', 'having shod', and 'having taken') Paul now uses the imperative *dexasthe*, meaning 'accept' or 'receive.' There is accordingly a shift here from dressing oneself in the virtues of truth, righteousness, readiness and faith to receiving a helmet from the Father. This helmet had the same function in relation to the mind as the breastplate had in relation to the heart. Indeed, if the breastplate is the Christian's heart-protector, the helmet is the

Christian's mind-protector.

This brings us to the phrase 'the helmet of salvation.' What did Paul mean by 'salvation' here? And what did he want his readers to do in the spiritual battle when he encouraged us to receive the helmet from God?

To answer this we must turn to the idea of salvation.

Paul has already used the language of salvation in Ephesians. In chapter 2 he begins by stressing what we have been saved from. He writes:

And you He made alive, who were dead in trespasses and sins, in which you once walked according to the course of this world, according to the prince of the power of the air, the spirit who now works in the sons of disobedience, among whom also we all once conducted ourselves in the lusts of our flesh, fulfilling the desires of the flesh and of the mind, and were by nature children of wrath, just as the others.

Here Paul emphasizes the tragic and terrifying situation of slavery before we encountered Christ and chose to put our faith in him. He talks about our former life as a life characterised by trespasses and sins, a life ruled by the devil, a life that made us sons of disobedience, a life that was surrendered to the lusts of the flesh, a life that meant that we were children of wrath (i.e. a people who deserved divine judgment not mercy).

Having told us the bad news, Paul now turns to the good news, marking the transition with the simple words 'but God,' emphasizing in that one phrase that it was God who took the initiative to save us.

But God, who is rich in mercy, because of His great love with which He loved us, even when we were dead in trespasses, made us alive together with Christ (by grace you have been saved), and raised us up together, and made us sit together in the heavenly places in Christ Jesus, that in the ages to come He might show the exceeding riches of His grace in His kindness toward us in Christ Jesus. For by grace you have been saved through faith, and that not of yourselves; it is the gift of God, not of works, lest anyone should boast.

Here Paul tells his readers that they couldn't pull themselves out of this dark and desperate plight by their own efforts. Rather, God himself initiated a rescue plan and he did this because of his rich love, great mercy and amazing grace. All these momentous, divine attributes were displayed 'in Christ Jesus'. By sending his only Son into the world to deal with our sins, God demonstrated the extreme lengths to which he was prepared to go to liberate us from our slavery to sin. All that a person needs to do to receive freedom is to accept that it is only by God's grace (in other words, by his acting in love on our behalf) that we are saved and then choose to enter into a relationship with Christ that results in us being seated with him in the heavenly realms.

This brings us to a truth that is extremely important and which has not been emphasized enough in Western theology. In Paul's mind, God's grace not only saves us FROM something. It also saves us TO something. God's grace saves us FROM slavery to sin. But we must also always remember that God's grace saves us TO a life of honoured sonship.

To underline this point, we must go back to the beginning of Ephesians where Paul embarks on a long and breathless eulogy of all that God has done for us in Christ. Using a Jewish form of prayer known as the *berakah*, Paul launches into his list of blessings by speaking eloquently and passionately about being chosen and adopted by God the Father:

Blessed be the God and Father of our Lord Jesus Christ, who has blessed us with every spiritual blessing in the heavenly places in Christ, just as He chose us in Him before the foundation of the world, that we should be holy and without blame before Him in love, having predestined us to adoption as sons by Jesus Christ to Himself, according to the good pleasure of His will, to the praise of the glory of His grace, by which He has made us accepted in the Beloved.

Notice here the reference to being 'predestined to adoption.' In Part 2 of Behold the Man we looked at Paul's understanding and deployment of the vital metaphor of adoption and his teaching about our status as sons. This metaphor has received insufficient attention until relatively recently but is now recognised to be central to Paul's theology of salvation. Let us remind ourselves briefly what Paul had in mind.

In the Roman practice of adoption, a slave's son was sometimes emancipated from a desperate and dangerous life by being purchased out of slavery. This act was performed by an adopting father who was unable to have children of his own and was eager to extend his *pater familias*. Once purchased out of slavery, the boy's previous debts were all cancelled and he was given the unearned privilege of a new father, a new freedom, a new family, and indeed a new fortune.

Applying this to the life of the Christian, Paul says that we too have been bought out of slavery. Our freedom from sin has not been purchased using money but rather with the blood of the Son of God. As a result we who were once living under the authority of a slave are now under the authority of the most perfect Father in the universe. We are members of a new family (the church), we enjoy a glorious freedom (from sin), and a heavenly fortune (our inheritance in Christ).

Seen in this light, salvation in Paul's mind involves a transition from slavery to sonship. For Paul, salvation is not just being saved FROM sin (the emphasis of so much Protestant preaching over the centuries). It is also being saved TO the life of a son. Thanks to the extreme measures taken by the One and Only Son by nature, we can be set free from our slavery to sin and become the royal, adopted sons and daughters of the King of Heaven.

This is a priceless privilege!

For a Christian to stand firm in the brutal onslaughts of the enemy in the spiritual warfare that rages on in the cosmos, the helmet of salvation is an absolute prerequisite. The effective Christian soldier needs to have his mind protected by the great truth that we have received salvation FROM sin and TO sonship. Half measures here are not enough. It is not sufficient to know that we have been saved from the shame of a sinful life. We must also know that we have been saved to the honour of being an adopted daughter or son of God the Father. Those who know such things in their redeemed and renewed minds live in a perpetual state of assurance that they are forgiven and indeed 'accepted in the Beloved.' Nothing can persuade them otherwise. Whatever the wicked one may throw at them, they stand securely in their honoured position in Christ and celebrate the certitude of their sonship.

Now all this is vital to recognize because the greatest battlefield is not some foreign landscape where soldiers clash but the landscape between our ears — namely our minds. This is where the evil one seeks to attack us most violently because he knows that the way a person thinks is everything. What I believe in my mind will dictate how I behave in my life. If the evil one can make me think like a slave again, then I will behave like a slave again. But if I intentionally guard my mind against such deception, then I can daily stand my ground and declare, 'I am a royal son of heaven by adoption and no strategy from the pit of hell or from the thoughts of men can ever remove that honour from my life.'

In saying this we see immediately the sense and indeed the urgency of Paul commanding his readers to receive the helmet of salvation. Salvation is something we receive. It is not something we earn. Furthermore, this salvation is received by faith and it is acknowledged and understood in a mind transformed and renewed by the Holy Spirit.

What Paul is therefore writing about here is the importance of having a mind-protector. He knows that the battle for the mind is fierce and unceasing. Even Jesus was assaulted in his mind when the devil taunted him saying, 'if you are the Son of God.' But Jesus was wearing the helmet of salvation. Facing the devil in the desert, Jesus cast his mind back to the revelation in the river. He protected his mind with the remembrance of the words, 'this is my beloved son.'

Protecting the mind is therefore vital for our victory. This is why Paul talks about the mind a number of times in Ephesians. In Ephesians 2.3 he speaks about how we fulfilled the desires of our minds before we were Christians (the word is *dianoia*, meaning 'mind, imagination, or understanding'). He uses the same word in Ephesians 4.13 when he describes how our understanding was darkened prior to our salvation. Now that we are in Christ, the eyes of our *dianoia*, our understanding, can be enlightened (Ephesians 1.18).

Perhaps the most detailed description of the mind-transforming implications of salvation is found in Ephesians 4:17-24:

This I say, therefore, and testify in the Lord, that you should no longer walk as the rest of the Gentiles walk, in the futility of their mind, having their understanding darkened, being alienated from the life of God, because of the ignorance that is in them, because of the hardening of their heart; who, being past feeling, have given themselves over to lewdness, to work all uncleanness with greediness. But you have not so learned Christ, if indeed you have heard Him and have been taught by Him, as the truth is in Jesus: that you put off, concerning your former conduct, the old man which grows corrupt according to the deceitful lusts, and be renewed in the spirit of your mind, and that you put on the new man which was created according to God, in true righteousness and holiness.

What an extraordinarily graphic description of the battle for the mind! This battle was fierce enough before we were in Christ but Paul makes it clear that it is just as ferocious if not more so now that we are in Christ. In Christ, we need to put on the helmet of salvation and recognize the full glory of our identity in the Beloved. In union with the Son by nature, we who are adopted sons and daughters not only put sin to death, we also experience the dynamic power of the resurrection. More glorious still, in Christ, we are elevated above the dark powers of the cosmos and are seated in the heavenly realms, empowered to live the ascended life.

This is the full inheritance of our adoption as sons and daughters and it is an inheritance that is only accessed by revelation. This is why Paul is so eager for his readers to know these truths and why he prays so earnestly for their minds to be spiritually illuminated. Listen to his prayer in Ephesians 1:18-21, a prayer that

the eyes of your understanding being enlightened; that you may know what is the hope of His calling, what are the riches of the glory of His inheritance in the saints, and what is the exceeding greatness of His power toward us who believe, according to the working of His mighty power which He worked in Christ when He raised Him from the dead and seated Him at His right hand in the heavenly places, far above all principality and power and might and dominion, and every name that is named, not only in this age but also in that which is to come.

Why is Paul so passionate that believers should understand such things? It is because he knows from his own experience that a Christian who understands who he really is also appreciates what he really has. Put another way, the greater our understanding of our position, the greater the release of spiritual power will be from our lives.

Putting on the helmet of salvation is therefore an essential daily discipline. Standing up in our belt and breastplate, wearing our shoes and carrying our shield, we remind ourselves – we RE-MIND or realign our thinking — of our position in Christ. We declare,

'I am no longer a slave to sin but a son. My old sinful life has been crucified in the death of Christ. I now live and operate in the same power that raised Christ Jesus from the dead. More than that, I am seated with the Ascended Lord in the heavenly realms. In him, I am more than an overcomer and victorious over every assault of the enemy. Thanks to what the Word of God teaches, I am fully persuaded that I am forgiven, accepted, and redeemed. Thanks to the work of the Holy Spirit in my life, I know by experience that I am beloved, chosen, adopted and special. I am honoured not ashamed. I am saved from slavery and I now enjoy the status of a son. Therefore I shall never be separated from the Father's love. These things are sealed upon my heart and inscribed upon my mind, which is being renewed in the Holy Spirit and protected by the helmet of salvation every day of my life.'

What would happen on the earth if every Christian man were to wake up today, put on the belt of truth and the breastplate of righteousness, the shoes of readiness and the shield of faith, and receive again by revelation — through the Word and the Spirit —

the wonderful truth that they are saved from slavery to sonship? Such men without doubt would have the capacity to stand firm in the battle and advance the Gospel of peace in the world. Such men would not doubt either their identity or their authority. They would know who they are in Christ and they would use what they have in Christ. They would appreciate their royal position and they would operate in their royal power and authority. In short, their minds would be transformed and their thinking sanctified.

How vital therefore is the helmet of salvation!

For a Christian man to conform to the image of Christ, this piece of armour must never be neglected and must ever be protected.

We have said throughout this book that manhood represents the interior life of a man while masculinity denotes the external contours of his behaviour.

For a man to be truly a man in the Christian sense, he must pay careful attention to his inner life – especially to his thought life. He must cultivate Christ-like thinking if he is to exhibit Christ-like conduct.

In this respect, the helmet of salvation is pivotal. When the Christian man places this helmet on his head, he reminds himself that he is saved from the shame of sin and saved to the honour of being a son. In the process, something dynamic and dramatic takes place in his manhood – in the interior life of his mind, understanding and imagination. He starts to see himself differently — as a son of the Most High God by gracious adoption. He is no longer a pauper, he is a prince. He is no longer a nobody, he is a somebody. He is no longer ordinary, he is extraordinary. As he realises these truths, he recognizes with the profoundest humility that this honour is not given to him because of his own achievements. Rather, he always remembers that this heavenly privilege is given to him because he is 'in Christ' and because of that he stands in the same position before the Father as the Eternal Son does. This honour is then received with gratitude and celebrated with joy. It is the wellspring of his private world which in turn produces a creative and God-glorifying overflow into his public world. Put another way, it is a redeemed manhood which is then expressed in an outwardly observable and Christ-like masculinity.

Christian men therefore have a mandate to place the helmet of salvation on their heads and to remember daily who they truly are in Christ.

They are sons, not slaves.

They are defined by their position, not their performance.

They do not achieve in order to be loved but they achieve because they are loved.

They relate to the Father as sons and they reign on the earth as servants.

Saved by grace alone through faith alone in Christ alone, they stand firm in the fight and win many skirmishes in the epic struggle against dark powers.

They always listen for the Father's voice while their swords beat against their shields — a voice that cries out from a torn heaven, 'you are my beloved son.'

Their helmets may be dented and battered in the battle, but they hold their heads high and their plumed feathers tremble marvellously in the wind of the Spirit.

In tight ranks with other such men, they advance *Pax Christiana* throughout the earth.

They are a band of brothers.

They are heaven's heroes.

They are real men.

BEHOLD THE MAN

Chapter 6:

THE SWORD OF THE SPIRIT

After encouraging his readers to receive the helmet of salvation, Paul now tells them to receive from God the sword of the Spirit.

When Paul mentions this sword, he has in mind the *gladius* of the Roman legionary. This was neither a long slashing sword nor a short stabbing sword. In the time of the Emperor Augustus the regulation Roman sword was between 40-56 centimetres long and it was eight centimetres wide across the shoulders. It had a wasp-waisted blade and a long tapering point. It weighed between 1.2 and 1.6 kilograms and was sheathed inside a tinned or silvered scabbard embossed with motifs celebrating Augustus' reign. Such swords were attached to the legionary's belt using a four ring suspension system. Senior officers and centurions wore their swords on the left of their body. The soldiers wore theirs on the right.

The legionary kept this weapon at his side at all times. He had regular training in swordsmanship and kept his blade clean and sharp. This weapon, designed for the cut and thrust of close quarter fighting, was usually employed after soldiers had hurled their spears at the enemy. Having caused death and confusion by a volley of missiles, the legionaries would charge into the ranks of dazed and dying enemy soldiers and finish them off with the sword. The sword was accordingly an offensive weapon.

With this in mind, let's look carefully at what Paul says.

First of all, we should pause and reflect on the metaphor of the sword itself. While Paul most likely has one eye on the Roman *gladius* there is also little doubt that he has the other fixed upon the Old Testament image of the Divine Warrior. One of the most notable pictures in this tradition can be found in Isaiah 27.1:

In that day the LORD with His severe sword, great and strong, will punish Leviathan the fleeing serpent, Leviathan that twisted serpent; and He will slay the reptile that is in the sea.

One thing worthy of mention from this passage is the description of the victim of God's sword. Isaiah tells us that it is Leviathan that will form the target of Yahweh's ire. Leviathan is a symbol of the devil (Job 41.1-11; Psalm 72.12-14; Isaiah 51.9; Ezekiel 29.3; Ezekiel 32.2; Revelation 12.3-4). What is important here is that it is the 'fleeing serpent' and not people who are destined for Yahweh's sword. This supports Paul's view that our enemies are principalities and powers not human beings. The metaphor of the sword, while having a clearly attacking and indeed lethal nuance, is therefore not meant to be taken literally nor is it intended to fuel aggression towards people. It is a spiritual weapon to be used in our corporate stand against the dark powers under the devil's control.

The second thing to note is that Paul calls this sword 'the sword of the Spirit.' In using this phrase it is not his intention to describe the Spirit as the source of the sword. Rather, Paul has in mind the efficacy of the sword rather than its origins. In other words, it is the Spirit — that is, the Holy Spirit — who makes the sword incisive in the battle. It is the Spirit who enables us to do damage to the enemy's ranks because it is the Spirit who makes the sword such a devastating, penetrating weapon against evil. With the sword, Christians can pierce the darkness.

The third thing we should understand is that Paul's phraseology is slightly different in relation to the sword from the other armour items. Let's remind ourselves of his description of the other pieces:

The belt of truth
The breastplate of righteousness
The shoes of the readiness of the gospel of peace
The shield of faith
The helmet of salvation

In each of these five descriptions the former represents the latter. In other words, the belt represents truth, the breastplate represents righteousness, the shoes represent readiness, and so on. Not so in the case of the sword. The sword of the Spirit does not represent the Spirit. Rather, the sword — which is 'of the Spirit' — represents the 'word of God.' We must accordingly take care not to think that Paul is using the same phraseology and thereby make the mistake of seeing the sword as the Spirit. This would be very dangerous. We cannot think or talk in terms of wielding the Spirit. The Holy Spirit is beyond our wielding. He is in fact beyond all forms of human manipulation. He is the unlimited and untameable power of the living God.

This brings us inevitably to a fourth question: if the sword represents 'the word of God' not the Spirit, then what did Paul mean by this? Some of us may be too quick to assume that Paul is thinking of what we would call 'the Bible' when he refers to 'the word of God.' In other words, we may assume that Paul is referring to the sixty six books of the canon of Scripture. But this is simplistic. The fact is not all of the books of the New Testament had been written by the time Paul told his readers to receive the sword of the Spirit, which is 'the word of God.' The New Testament had not been formed and some of its documents had not yet been written. To interpret the 'word of God' as simply the Christian's Bible may therefore not be completely accurate.

So what does it mean? When Paul speaks of the 'word' he uses the Greek term *rhema*. This word is used 73 times in the New Testament. Another term that Paul uses and which is translated as 'word' is the Greek noun logos. It has often been taught over the last fifty years or so that these two terms are not synonyms but are used in distinctive ways and with different meanings in the New Testament. Many have contended that logos refers to the written word (i.e. to the Scriptures) while *rhema* refers to the spoken word (i.e. to prophetic utterances or confessions of faith). If this is true, then wielding the sword of the Spirit would refer to the Spirit-inspired release of a spoken word in a particular situation.

This is not the time or the place to go into a full-blown debate about the *Logos-Rhema* controversy. Suffice it to say that the often claimed distinction between these two words simply doesn't hold water. If we take an example from Ephesians itself, Paul says in chapter 1 and verse 13, 'in Him you also trusted, after you heard the word (logos) of truth, the gospel of your salvation.' No one can really doubt that Paul is referring to the spoken word when he uses logos in this context. The use of the verb 'heard' in relation to logos, not to mention the connection between hearing the logos and hearing the 'gospel of your salvation', proves conclusively and comprehensively that logos in Paul can refer to a spoken word.

A further piece of evidence can be found in John 4.50 – the story of the healing of the noble official's son. Note what the storyteller records, 'the man believed the word [logos] that Jesus spoke to him and went on his way.' Here *logos* refers not to a written word in the Bible but to a spoken word. *Logos* and *rhema* can sometimes therefore refer to the exact opposite of what some claim.

One final example should confirm the strength of this argument. In 1 Peter 1.23, Peter says that Christians are reborn through 'the word of God that lives and abides forever.' Here he uses logos. When he completes this thought a few verses later he states that 'the word of the LORD endures forever.' Here he uses the word rhema. For Peter, the two words are interchangeable.

And we would argue the same for Paul. We have just seen how he uses logos in Ephesians 1.13 in a context which clearly alludes to words that were spoken. Later on in Ephesians (in 5.26) he says this:

Husbands, love your wives, just as Christ also loved the church and gave Himself for her, that He might sanctify and cleanse her with the washing of water by the word.

Here Paul uses *rhema* in a context where the proponents of what has been called 'rhematology' would expect logos. We cannot therefore escape the conclusion that in the New Testament (as in the Greek translation of the Old Testament known as the Septuagint, or LXX for short) *logos* and *rhema* are not words with distinctive meanings. They are synonyms.

If we return then to 'the sword of the Spirit, which is the word of God,' we propose that Paul is not referring to the applied use of written Scripture, nor is he referring to the prophetic use of spoken utterances. As much as we might like Paul to say this we cannot and must not make him.

So what did Paul mean by 'the word of God' when he spoke about the sword? It is our contention that in this context it means giving bold and loving utterance to the Gospel of peace. What is it that Paul asks his readers to pray for at the end of this great exhortation in Ephesians 6.10-20? He asks in Ephesians 6:19 that they pray

For me, that utterance may be given to me, that I may open my mouth boldly to make known the mystery of the gospel, for which I am an ambassador in chains; that in it I may speak boldly, as I ought to speak.

It seems to us that this provides a vital clue to understanding what is meant by taking the sword of the Spirit, which is the word of God. To receive this sword is to receive the word of God which is the Gospel of peace, the gospel of salvation, the message of truth. It is to accept it as God's good news designed and destined to bring people into a radical peace both with God and with each other. The proclamation of this 'good news' of peace — of these glad tidings of shalom — is a task for which we must all be trained and it is a mandate which all men must be ready to fulfil. When we make a stand together for the Gospel of peace we raise our swords and pierce the present darkness.

What happens when this Gospel, this 'word of God', is proclaimed and demonstrated in the power of the Spirit? Two things at least occur, and they are dynamic.

The first is that the spiritual blindness of unbelievers is confronted. The preaching of the message of the Gospel is incisive and decisive, penetrating through the defences of peoples' rebellious minds and hard hearts. As the writer to the Hebrews puts it,

The word of God is living and powerful, and sharper than any

two-edged sword, piercing even to the division of soul and spirit, and of joints and marrow, and is a discerner of the thoughts and intents of the heart.

Raising the sword means giving voice to the Gospel of peace in such an anointed way that unbelievers come to experience an agonizing and piercing conviction of sin. There is simply nowhere left to hide. The eyes of God are upon them.

Raising the sword — when that sword is sharpened and applied by the Spirit of God — therefore brings listeners to a place of repentance and faith. This is why Paul can reminisce with his church in Thessalonica about what happened when he raised the sword of the Spirit and pierced their hearts with the preaching of the Gospel:

Our gospel did not come to you in word only, but also in power, and in the Holy Spirit and in much assurance, as you know what kind of men we were among you for your sake. And you became followers of us and of the Lord, having received the word in much affliction, with joy of the Holy Spirit...

[1 Thessalonians 1.5-6].

See how Paul emphasizes two things here. He emphasizes that the message was delivered under the anointing of the Spirit. In other words, the sword that was raised was not the sword of man but the sword of the Spirit. He secondly emphasizes that when this sword was raised it brought 'much affliction.' In other words, there was plenty of godly sorrow before there was an outbreak of joy in the Holy Spirit. There was much repentance before there was extravagant rejoicing.

The first thing that happens when we raise the sword is that the darkness is lifted from peoples' minds and the hardness is softened in peoples' hearts. Preaching the Gospel of peace therefore releases people from the strong holds that the enemy has had over their fallen minds and hearts. It brings illumination to minds which the god of this age (i.e. Satan) has darkened (2 Corinthians 4.3-4). As such, proclaiming the Gospel of peace is a lethal, mighty, spiritual weapon (2 Corinthians 10.3-6). It is not a defensive weapon. It is very much a weapon of attack against those satanically inflicted mindsets and ideologies which set themselves up hubristically against the knowledge of God and which hold them captive.

The second thing that happens when the sword is raised is that the principalities and powers which lie behind these atheistic and even anti-theistic ways of thinking come under judgment. Now in a sense they have already been judged at the Cross. As Paul says in Colossians 2.15: 'having disarmed principalities and powers, He made a public spectacle of them, triumphing over them in it' (i.e. in his death on the Cross). The sentence has already been passed on these dark powers at Calvary. But every time the sword is raised and the Gospel of peace is proclaimed, these sinister principalities and powers are reminded of their past judgment as men and women find peace with God and with each other at the foot of the Cross. As this happens, the powers feel the penetrating thrust of the sword of the Spirit. Indeed, whenever a lost soul finds peace with God these powers are reminded of both their past defeat and their future destruction. Every time the Gospel brings a miraculous unity between warring brothers and sisters, or between nations and tribes, the divisive powers experience the tip of God's blade. One day, of course, they will be terminated by the sharp two-edged sword of Christ's mouth forever (Revelation 1.16; 2.12).

Perhaps now we can see why it is so important for us to interpret the 'sword of the Spirit, which is the word of God,' in a responsible way. In its original context, it is hard to see how it could mean receiving and applying a Bible verse or a sudden revelation. It actually means something much more dynamic than either of these things. It means making a stand and sharing the Gospel in an anointed way in a situation where people need to find peace with God and peace with each other.

The word of God in this context is accordingly what Paul earlier in Ephesians calls 'the word of truth, the gospel of salvation.'

Underline the phrase, 'the gospel of salvation.' The Gospel that we are called to preach is not a Gospel of fulfilment. It is a Gospel of salvation. This point is extremely important in the present Western world, where many churches have morphed the Gospel of salvation into a message of how Christians can fulfil their potential. However much the Gospel of salvation leads a person to find their true purpose — and it surely does — this is not the main theme of the authentic Gospel. Paul's Gospel is a Gospel of peace. It is the good news that Jesus Christ – who is Son of God, Lord, Peace Bringer, Saviour and the Coming King — has reconciled us to the Father and to each other through his self-giving death on a Roman cross. It is the glad tidings that peace has been secured in our relationship with the Father and with each other and this not through exercising brute force but through absorbing it in loving and non-violent resistance.

This Gospel of peace, also known as the Gospel of salvation, is a message which does not hold back on the wilful self-rule and rebellion which made this sacrificial death necessary — a self-rule which Paul calls 'sin.' In fact, Paul goes to some lengths in his description of what we human beings have all needed saving from:

And you He made alive, who were dead in trespasses and sins, in which you once walked according to the course of this world, according to the prince of the power of the air, the spirit who now works in the sons of disobedience, among whom also we all once conducted ourselves in the lusts of our flesh, fulfilling the desires of the flesh and of the mind, and were by nature children of wrath, just as the others

[Ephesians 2.1-3]

In Ephesians 4.17-20, Paul goes even further in his portrayal of the state from which we have been saved:

This I say, therefore, and testify in the Lord, that you should no longer walk as the rest of the Gentiles walk, in the futility of their mind, having their understanding darkened, being alienated from the life of God, because of the ignorance that is in them, because of the hardening of their heart; who, being past feeling, have given themselves over to lewdness, to work all uncleanness with greediness.

This kind of discourse is the furthest remove from the Gospel of fulfilment, with all its talk of 'fulfilling your potential' and 'seizing your destiny.' Such things form part of the rewards of our salvation but they cannot be fully realised in our lives unless we confront the harsh reality of life lived under our own rule rather than the reign of God in Christ. If we don't help people to see the full agony of what life is like for them as a spiritual orphan how will we ever persuade them of their need for spiritual adoption by the perfect Father? It makes no sense at all. A person must know and recognize their orphan state if they are going to long to be rescued from it. A person must come to their senses and see that they are living in the far country if they are to want to come running home to the Father's house. A person must fully acknowledge — with a reality check known in the Bible as repentance — that they are separated from the love of all loves if they are to ache in their hearts for a homecoming. This is a vital part of the Gospel imperative.

For Paul, standing in the full armour of God means, among other things, raising and wielding the sword of the Spirit, which is the word of God. This word that we are called to use has not lost any of its sharpness or its cutting edge. It is a message of salvation more than a message of fulfilment. It is a message of urgency not a message of triviality. It is a message that brings peace.

Christian men in this generation need to raise a battle cry for the true Gospel of salvation. They may need to learn to speak in a new idiom to touch those around them, but they must not dilute or pollute the Gospel of peace in the process. They must be prepared in any and every given situation to take their swords from their sheaths and raise it up for Jesus Christ — God's Son, Lord of lords, and Saviour. With the help of the Holy Spirit, they will be enabled to use their swords in such a way that spiritual darkness is pierced and rebel defences are penetrated. This is the significance of the sword of the Spirit, the word of God. Whether at home, in the workplace, in prison, politics, or in the pulpit, the Christian man is called to be the carrier of the Good News of Christ's hard-earned *shalom* into his sphere of influence, changing the atmosphere around him from enmity and hostility to peace and unity. Nothing makes the devil madder than this. He detests it when his divisive strategies are exposed and defeated by sword-wielding men of God. He hates the sight of the gleaming blade of God, wielded by Christian men who are no longer weaklings but warriors.

For this to become an increasing reality, Christian men must understand that wielding the sword is not the calling of the preacher alone but the calling of every man in Christ. When Paul tells his readers to put on the armour pieces, he is not talking to preachers but to everyone. He uses 'you' plural in these verses in Ephesians 6.14-16. 'All of you take up the sword.' It is simply no good then for Christian men to say that being a bearer of the Good News of peace is the responsibility of the evangelist or the pastor. It is a mandate for every man in Christ. All of us need to learn to take our swords from their scabbards, to raise it with other men, and to thrust its penetrating blade into those powers that keep people in enmity when they could be living in harmony with God and each other.

This means that the Christian man must be prepared to bring out their swords whenever it is needed. They cannot just go to church once a week and settle for seeing someone else wield their spiritual sword in the pulpit. Their own swords must be brought out and used on a daily basis. And they need to be used in close quarter interaction with people whose minds have been darkened by the powers and whose orphan hearts have become hostile to God and one another.

Here we need to remember that Paul uses the metaphor of the sword because this is a weapon intended for close combat. If Paul had been thinking of long distance warfare he would have said, 'take up the spear of the Spirit, which is the word of God.' But he was not. He was thinking of direct communication with people who are under the influence of hostile powers. He was envisaging face-to-face dialogue in which the man of war — at enmity with God and others — is disarmed by the incisive power of the man bearing the Gospel of peace.

Perhaps we need an example here. One of the most remarkable Vicars in the Church of England is Canon Andrew White, also known as The Vicar of Bagdad. Andrew has always had a great love for the Middle East. When he was told that he was too sick to work as a Vicar in England (he has multiple sclerosis), Andrew decided to move to Iraq and become the Vicar of St George's Bagdad. Since that time he has built one of the most exceptional churches in one of the ugliest and most terrible situations. St George's has a congregation of thousands, including Muslims. It also has a huge feeding and relief programme, as well as one of the largest health clinics in Iraq. The congregation has set up a school which is not only available to children who go to the church but also to others of whatever faith. With education as hard to find as good medicine, St George's provides an extraordinary service to its war torn city.

When Andrew is not serving his congregation he is either acting in his role as chaplain to the US embassy or serving the Iraqi government. His main role in that second capacity is to work as a religious leader among mainly Muslim religious leaders to work for peace and reconciliation. In fact, Andrew has been directly involved in international reconciliation and conflict resolution for a long time, not least between Arabs and Israelis. He has consistently and courageously brought the Gospel of peace to the Middle East. In Iraq, thousands have found peace with God and with each other through his radical, Gospel ministry.

For years Andrew has worked at close quarters with dictators and terrorists, bringing the peace of God into the most hostile contexts. He has witnessed the glory of God manifested in the most heart-breaking and tragic situations. He has seen the sick healed and dead people raised. The children in his church have had visions of Jesus and sing with great conviction and hope, 'soon and very soon we are going to see the King.' Andrew describes St George's as 'the happiest church he has ever seen'.

Andrew has fifteen medals all awarded to him as international peace prizes. He at one time ran the religious track of the peace process designed to bring reconciliation between Arabs and Israelis. Today he runs the high council of religious leaders in Iraq, working with the Iraqi government to bring peace and reconciliation between Shiites and Sunnis. He has been and continues to be a friend of Presidents, Prime Ministers and leading politicians in many countries. His longing is to see people stop killing each other and his ministry is based around loving one's enemies and healing the sick, both of which were commanded by the Lord Jesus himself. Above all, he helps people who are at war with each other to listen to one another. As Andrew has said:

"What you do first, is you get them to listen to each other... And that's a very long process. The American poet Longfellow said 'Who is my enemy? It is the person whose story I have not heard'. So often we begin by just hearing each other's stories."

We have included this brief description of 'the Vicar of Bagdad' to underline a number of vital points in this chapter about the sword of the Spirit.

The first is that wielding this sword means close quarter interaction with people who are at enmity with God and with each other. It is not a long distance ministry.

Secondly, using this sword is not to be understood in an aggressive, militaristic way. It is meant to be understood in terms of loving and serving others.

Thirdly, however war-like the image of sword-bearing may seem, Paul understands the use of this sword as a peace-making act — as an act of supernatural reconciliation.

Fourthly, bringing an end to war between people can only happen when people first find peace with God. Churches like St George's showcase this.

Finally, given that it is peace with God first, peace with each other second, the Christian man must be committed to presenting the gospel of salvation.

Isn't it time that we received from our Heavenly Father the sword of the spirit?

Isn't it time that God's sons started to bring incisive, peace-making words into hostile situations?

Isn't it time for Christian men to open their mouths and speak kindly but courageously the Good News about Jesus?

Chapter 7:

PRAYING IN THE SPIRIT

Christian men are called to be men of prayer, simple as that. We are called to be men who enjoy intimate communion with the Father as his royally adopted sons. We are called to pray for ourselves and for others for an increasing knowledge — both cognitive and affectionate — of our Heavenly Father and the glorious inheritance he has given to us in his Son. We are called to be princes who boldly approach the King's throne and pray for the advancement of the Kingdom of heaven on earth through the clear and courageous preaching of the Gospel of peace. This is the destiny of the true man of God – to stand and pray in the presence of the Holy Spirit. For the Christian warrior, prayer is a vital and indispensible weapon.

With that in mind it is no surprise to find that the Apostle Paul rounds off his teaching on spiritual warfare with a call to prayer.

Prayer is in fact very much at the heart of Paul's Letter to the Ephesians.

He starts the letter with a prayer of thanksgiving:

Blessed be the God and Father of our Lord Jesus Christ, who has blessed us with every spiritual blessing in the heavenly places in Christ.

[Ephesians 1.3]

He adds that he continually thinks of the congregation in Ephesus and prays for them earnestly:

I also, after I heard of your faith in the Lord Jesus and your love for all the saints, do not cease to give thanks for you, making mention of you in my prayers.

[Ephesians 1.15-16]

In the centre of his letter, he returns to the subject of prayer, this time modelling to his spiritual children how they should pray:

I bow my knees to the Father of our Lord Jesus Christ, from whom the whole family in heaven and earth is named, that He would grant you, according to the riches of His glory, to be strengthened with might through His Spirit in the inner man.

[Ephesians 3:14-16]

Now at the conclusion of his letter, Paul returns to the subject of prayer, telling his readers to receive the sword of the Spirit, adding

praying always with all prayer and supplication in the Spirit, being watchful to this end with all perseverance and supplication for all the saints — and for me, that utterance may be given to me, that I may open my mouth boldly to make known the mystery of the gospel, for which I am an ambassador in chains; that in it I may speak boldly, as I ought to speak.

[Ephesians 6:17-20]

See how prayer lies at the beginning, middle and end of Paul's letter. In Paul's mind, prayer must be the highest priority at the start, the middle and the conclusion of one's tasks. Just as the Jewish man prayed at three set times each day — at dawn, noon and night — so Paul, in a thoroughly Jewish way, beckons to his readers to make sure that their lives are begun, sustained and ended in prayer.

Prayer is accordingly a key theme in Paul's letter.

And it is a fitting conclusion to Paul's passage about the spiritual war in Ephesians 6.10-20.

If we look closely at how Paul designs this section we can see once again that he is thinking in threes.

The start of the call to arms involves a description of the spiritual battle itself, in verses 10-13:

Finally, my brethren, be strong in the Lord and in the power of His might. Put on the whole armor of God, that you may be able to stand against the wiles of the devil. For we do not wrestle against flesh and blood, but against principalities, against powers, against the rulers of the darkness of this age, against spiritual hosts of wickedness in the heavenly places. Therefore take up the whole armor of God, that you may be able to withstand in the evil day, and having done all, to stand.

The second section (verses 14-16) describes the six main pieces of armour in the Christian soldier's panoply:

Stand therefore, having girded your waist with truth, having put on the breastplate of righteousness, and having shod your feet with the preparation of the gospel of peace; above all, taking the shield of faith with which you will be able to quench all the fiery darts of the wicked one. And take the helmet of salvation, and the sword of the Spirit, which is the word of God.

Now in the third section Paul turns his attention to the subject of prayer as he asks his readers to be watchful and to pray in the Spirit with all kinds of prayer for all the saints (i.e. for all Christian believers) and especially for him in his preaching of the Gospel. He asks specifically for boldness in preaching the Gospel. Put another way, he asks to be given courage in raising the sword of the Spirit and declaring the word of God, the Gospel of peace.

In light of the warfare context, it is interesting to ask the question, 'why does Paul not have prayer represented by a piece of the soldier's armour? He has done this for every other virtue, why not for prayer?'

This becomes even more interesting when we recall that there is one item in the Roman panoply which is very noticeable for its absence. This is the spear. In Paul's day, the Roman legionary's principal weapon was not in fact his sword but his *pilum* or spear. In his description of the panoply quoted earlier, Polybius spends much more time describing the legionary's spear than his sword.

He says that this weapon was like a moderately sized hunting spear with a barbed iron head fixed to the haft with numerous rivets, making it nearly impossible for it to become detached. The legionaries used to throw these *pila* like missiles into the air and towards the ranks of the enemy in front of them, causing carnage. They would then dash into the disorganised and devastated ranks and put their enemies to the sword.

Given that the *pilum* is effectively an airborne missile, it might seem strange to us that Paul does not follow his exhortation to take the sword with a call to 'pick up and hurl the missile of prayer!' Surely this was a golden opportunity to round off his teaching on the armour of God with a seventh and climactic metaphor (seven in Judaism is the number of perfection, after all).

For some this might be proof that Paul was not thinking of the Roman legionary at all when he spoke about the armour of God. It is important to mention very briefly here that there are some scholars who propose that Paul was not thinking of the Roman panoply in Ephesians 6.10-20 but referring instead to phrases from passages about Yahweh as the Divine Warrior in the Greek translation of the Old Testament (known as the LXX or the Septuagint). They argue that the background for Paul's language is in fact the armour pieces belonging to Yahweh which we find in Old Testament texts. The absence of the spear would just confirm for them that Paul's eyes are firmly fixed on a Hebraic tradition not on the Roman legionary.

However, this cannot really be sustained for two reasons. The first is because Paul clearly knows about the Roman panoply because he shows an awareness not only of the items of the Roman soldier's kit but also his battle tactics, such as the way the legionary was able to extinguish flame-tipped arrows by soaking the front of his shield in water before the battle. This unmistakable allusion to a Roman military strategy highlights that this is the primary background for the armour of God passage.

Secondly, we know that Paul was a Roman citizen and that he was more than familiar with Roman culture. When he speaks about our spiritual adoption it is obvious to the majority of scholars that he has his eyes fixed on Roman practices of adoption. There were no rites of adoption in the Jewish culture. There is no Old Testament teaching on how to adopt a child either. While Paul saw hints about our spiritual adoption in the Hebrew Bible, it was the Roman custom that primarily influenced his thinking.

For these two reasons then we propose that Paul is thinking primarily about the Roman panoply in Ephesians 6 and secondarily of the few Old Testament texts where Yahweh is portrayed as a warrior in heavenly armour.

This brings us right back to the conundrum mentioned earlier: why does Paul not enlist the metaphor of the spear when he concludes with an exhortation to pray?

The answer is intriguing.

If you look closely at Paul's language about prayer in verses 18-20 in Ephesians 6 there is one thing that may strike you and that is the positive way in which Paul describes intercessory prayer. For him, prayer is not about counter-acting negative, hostile forces. It is about giving support to positive advances of the Gospel.

Put simply, in Paul's mind prayer is interceding FOR not interceding AGAINST.

In Paul's theology of intercession, prayer is manifestly not about attacking the dark powers and principalities that govern the governments, as it were. It is not a matter of praying AGAINST wicked hosts, demonic strongholds or so-called territorial spirits (a phrase that has gained increasing traction in recent years). There is not a single hint anywhere in Paul's writing that prayer consists of throwing metaphorical missiles at the powers arraigned against us. There is certainly no hint of any suggestion that we are called to throw intercessory spears at the devil either. Rather, in Paul's writings, prayer is prayer FOR something, not prayer AGAINST. It is a positive enterprise not a negative one.

Perhaps this is the place to say something more generally about Paul's philosophy. The truth is that Paul does not write to his congregations and encourage them to be defined by what they are against. Quite the opposite, he writes and exhorts them to be known by what they are for.

When it comes to the Roman Emperor for example, Paul nowhere advocates that his spiritual sons and daughters spend their time going around saying that Caesar is not Lord. He tells them simply to state the positive — that Jesus Christ is Lord. He stresses what they are for not what they are against.

This mindset is carried over into Paul's theology and practice of prayer. He does not pray against the principalities and powers of the Empire even though these are the dark forces used by the evil one and against which we wrestle. Rather, he teaches us to use prayer in an altogether different way.

There are three things that are noteworthy about Paul's call to prayer in Ephesians 6.18-20.

The first is that this kind of praying should be pneumatic. The Greek word pneuma can be translated 'spirit.' Paul says that we are to pray 'in the Spirit,' (*en peneumati*) referring to the Holy Spirit. The Holy Spirit is in fact the interceding Spirit (Romans 8.27). Through the Spirit, we are joined to the intercession of the Son of God at the Father's throne (Romans 8.34). The role of the Holy Spirit can therefore never be underemphasized. Rather than focusing on demonic spirits in prayer, Paul focuses on the Holy Spirit. For him it is absolutely imperative that we yield in our own prayer life to the intercession of the Holy Spirit, whose sighs and groans within us are evidence that we have been connected to the passionate praying of the Son before his loving Father in heaven (Romans 8.26). Spirit-empowered prayer is therefore the priority. We have to earnestly seek the leading of the Holy Spirit whenever we pray.

The second thing to say is that this kind of prayer should be unrelenting. Paul calls Christian soldiers to engage in watchful and persevering prayer (Colossians 4:2). The Christian soldier keeps the watch and prays. He asks for the anointing of the Holy Spirit and prays without ceasing for the breakthrough in any given situation. He does not falter and he does not quit. He goes on praying as the Spirit guides him until the Spirit says 'it is finished.' In the spiritual battle, prayer — whatever form it takes in any individual's life, intercession or petition (Ephesians 6.18) — must be unrelenting. Perseverance is paramount.

Thirdly, the kind of prayer Paul is talking about needs to be focused. In Ephesians 6.18-20 Paul starts with a broad canvas but narrows down to a very precise focus. He begins with a call to intercede 'for all the saints', — that is, for those who are in Christ on the earth. He then homes in on his own need — the need to preach the Gospel boldly.

Notice the word Paul uses here which is translated 'boldly.' It is the Greek word *parresia*. This is exactly the same word that is used by Luke in Acts 4.31. In that passage we find the earliest, persecuted church praying to the Sovereign Lord of the Universe that he would give them all boldness and that he would also stretch out his hand to perform signs and wonders. The answer comes immediately with a dramatic manifestation of the presence of the Spirit and an instant and overwhelming empowering to speak *parresia* or boldly. This in turn launches the church into a new phase of effectiveness in mission as the believers preach the message of the Gospel with miracles accompanying and accrediting it.

This is the focus of true intercession. We do not pray AGAINST anything or anyone. Such an activity is the furthest remove from Paul's theology and practice. Instead, we pray FOR those things that will advance the Good News that Christ through his death has brought peace to the planet and salvation to the world. We pray for the ability to speak *parresia*, with courage, clarity and conviction. As someone once said, 'a belief is something you hold; a conviction is something that holds you.' Oh how we need Christian men of conviction — men who are empowered with supernatural boldness and who feel compelled to proclaim in words and demonstrate in works of power the Good News that Jesus is Lord!

For that to happen, someone somewhere needs to pray.

Let us return then to the issue of the spear. Why does Paul not call us to raise and hurl the spear of prayer?

Why does he show such restraint in this passage, when it would have been all too easy to mention a seventh piece of Roman military kit?

Why does he not complete the Roman panoply?

The answer is because prayer is not hurling curses against powers, people or places. Rather, prayer is interceding and petitioning in the Spirit for those God-given blessings that will lead to the Gospel being understood, declared, confirmed and advanced in the world.

Prayer is therefore a discipline with a positive focus.

And this is visible throughout Ephesians as a whole.

Look at what Paul stresses about prayer.

First of all, let's remember that prayer for Paul is about intimacy. For him, prayer is loving communion with Abba, Father. Prayer is conversation between adopted sons and daughters and their heavenly Papa. Prayer, as Paul puts it in Ephesians 3.14, is a matter of bowing the knee before the Father. It is about relationship — intimate friendship with Father God, in Christ, through the power of the Holy Spirit. In Christ, everyone can access to Abba, Father (Ephesians 2.18). Paul longs for all of us to understand that prayer is therefore love on its knees. This is why he prays for his congregation in Ephesus that they might come to know the inexhaustible dimensions of the divine love.

This brings us to a second positive focus and that has to do with insight. Paul knows that adopted children in the Roman world became the legitimate heirs of their father's estate. Inheritance was therefore a big deal. Newly adopted children found themselves receiving both now and in the future glorious riches that they simply hadn't earned or deserved. For Paul, this idea is carried over into the Christian life. Once we were orphans but now we are sons by adoption and as sons we are heirs — in fact, co-heirs with Jesus. For us to receive the full glory of this inheritance we must have insight into the legacy left to us through the finished work of the Cross. This is why Paul says in Ephesians 1.15-19,

I also, after I heard of your faith in the Lord Jesus and your love

for all the saints, do not cease to give thanks for you, making mention of you in my prayers: that the God of our Lord Jesus Christ, the Father of glory, may give to you the spirit of wisdom and revelation in the knowledge of Him, the eyes of your understanding being enlightened; that you may know what is the hope of His calling, what are the riches of the glory of His inheritance in the saints, and what is the exceeding greatness of His power toward us who believe.

See how positive Paul's focus is in these verses! He is praying FOR not AGAINST. He is asking that the adopted sons and daughters of God will know a deeper revelation of their Heavenly Father (that's intimacy) and that they will have a complete grasp of what is theirs in Christ. Here he is praying for insight, insight about the inheritance coming to the believer in the present and future tenses of their lives. This is why in Ephesians 3.17-19 he prays 'that you, being rooted and grounded in love, may be able to comprehend with all the saints what is the width and length and depth and height — to know the love of Christ which passes knowledge; that you may be filled with all the fullness of God.'

Paul's second great focus is therefore insight and this insight is inextricably related to his first focus which is intimacy. The reason these two are related has to do with Paul's understanding of how we know God. For him, knowing is personal not propositional, relational not religious, intimate not intellectual. In the Hebrew world, the verb 'to know' (*yada*) did not primarily have a cognitive or conceptual connotation. Rather, it had the connotation of intimate relationship. So in Paul's mind, the work of the Cross and the work of the Spirit have made it possible for us to know the Father intimately. In that intimacy — and only in that intimacy — true insight can be found.

But it doesn't end here. Paul has a third positive focus in mind. This we can call inroads. Paul prays for his spiritual children to grow in their intimacy with God and that they may have insight (arising from intimacy) into their true inheritance in Christ. This in turn leads to making inroads into the world through the proclamation of the Gospel of peace with signs and wonders following.

The reason why Paul prays for inroads, and indeed asks his readers to do the same, is because this is the right and natural overflow from intimacy and insight. The man who falls in love with God and begins to marvel at all that he has in Christ cannot help but share such glorious truths with others. This is much too good to be kept to oneself. He has to speak of it. As a newly adopted son, rescued from a hopeless orphanage, he is desperate to find other spiritual orphans and introduce them to his new, perfect, older brother — Jesus Christ. 'Here,' he cries, 'let me tell you about the brother you didn't know you had, the brother who is your best friend, the brother who gave his life for you, the brother who loves you like no other brother ever could.' That is Good News! It is the gospel of salvation.

Then, beyond that, the newly adopted son says this: 'your new brother wants to lead you home from the far country into the arms of the Father you've been looking for all your life — the Father whose love is as vast as the ocean and as limitless as the heavens. Come to Jesus, your brother, and you'll be given the honour of adoption. Then you will be a son not a slave and you'll find peace in the Father's house and joy in the Father's arms.'

Finally, the same newly adopted son adds this, 'and you'll find that you have a new family of adopted brothers and sisters. It's called the church, and its unity and diversity are unparalleled.'

One cannot deny that this is positive! Paul's prayer life embraced a cycle of intimacy, insight and inroads. He prayed for his readers to have increasing intimacy because he knew that this would lead to increasing insight which would in turn result inevitably in increasing inroads:

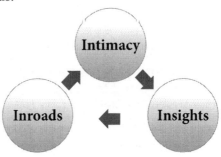

The reason Paul knew that inroads were an inevitable overflow from intimacy and insights is because one of the consequences of knowing God personally and receiving his inheritance was that the Christian would experience the empowering presence of God. This is why Paul prays that his readers will come to know 'what is the exceeding greatness of His power toward us who believe, according to the working of His mighty power which He worked in Christ when He raised Him from the dead and seated Him at His right hand in the heavenly places, far above all principality and power and might and dominion, and every name that is named, not only in this age but also in that which is to come' (Ephesians 1.19-21).

Paul rejoices in this fact, that positive prayer releases a greater awareness of the extraordinary supernatural power available to those who are in Christ. This is the same power that raised Jesus Christ from the dead and elevated him to the throne of God in heaven. That same death-defeating power is available to us as part of our inheritance as adopted sons and daughters. With this power at work within the church, inroads can be made that are never the product of our natural resources alone but are instead the result of the resurrection power of God at work. When such power is displayed, spiritual orphans find peace with God and peace with each other. The sick are healed, the oppressed are set free, the poor are blessed and the dead are raised. Instead of an Empire being extended through brute force, the Kingdom of heaven is advanced through the proclamation and demonstration of the Gospel of peace.

This is a positive vision!

And this is prayer!

Paul begins his letter by saying, 'I'm praying for you.' He ends it by saying, 'now please pray for me.'

For Paul, even though the world is a battleground not a playground, he doesn't call us to pray against the enemy.

He calls us to pray for each other, that we would enjoy increasing intimacy, insight and inroads.

In a church where it is predominantly the daughters of God

who travail in prayer, the sons need to catch this vision.

Prayer is for men as well as women.

And prayer is not throwing spears into the hordes of hell and its Satanic general.

It is an intimate communion and loving conversation with our heavenly Father.

It is the act in which we receive increasing insight into the mystery of the Gospel and the riches of our inheritance.

It is the source of our spiritual power and strength as we stand in the battle.

And it is the means by which we call out to the Commander of heaven's army on behalf of a brother or brothers who need reinforcements, supplies, protection or intervention.

With that in mind, we want to conclude this chapter with a prayer for Christian men to pray every day.

The Celtic Christians believed in praying what are known as 'dressing prayers.' These prayers were prayed by the Christian as he got up in the morning. One of the best known of these is Saint Patrick's Breastplate from (most likely) the eighth century. This was later transformed into a hymn which begins with the following stanza:

I bind unto myself today
The strong Name of the Trinity,
By invocation of the same
The Three in One and One in Three.

In the following pages, we offer our own dressing prayer for the man who desires to make a firm stand in the spiritual battle, dressed in the panoply of the spiritual legionary.

This prayer is a dressing prayer; it takes the virtues of truth telling, right living, readiness, faith, salvation and the word of God and makes them the focus of each petition.

May this dressing prayer bring you many victories!

ARMOUR DRESSING PRAYER

Dear Lord and heavenly Father,

I commit myself this day to stand firm in the spiritual battle and to remain faithful to your Son, the Lord Jesus Christ.

I bind unto myself the belt of truth, covenanting with you, my heavenly Father, to make the true truth of Jesus Christ central to my life and to be a truthful person and a truth-teller in every circumstance.

I place the breastplate over my chest and dedicate my heart to living in a right relationship with you, to behaving in the righteous way that Jesus would want, and respecting and promoting the rights of the oppressed.

I take the shoes of preparation and put them on my feet, promising to be ready in every situation to turn my armour against the enemy not against my family, my friends or my workmates, and thereby to promote peace.

I place the helmet of salvation on my head and celebrate the wonderful fact that I have been saved from being enslaved to sin and saved to the glorious freedom of being a son, and I ask you to renew my mind with this truth.

I receive from you the shield of faith and I believe in my heart and declare with my mouth that Jesus alone is the Son of God, my Lord, Saviour of the world, the Prince of Peace, and the Coming King.

I also receive the sword and promise to speak incisively, under the anointing of the Holy Spirit, about the glorious Good News about Jesus, and how he makes peace between us and God, and between each other, at the Cross.

I commit myself, Abba Father, to standing as a soldier and a son, in the full armour that you provide.

With my brothers in Christ, I vow not to falter or fall today but to be faithful and true to you.

And I ask for the resurrection power of your Holy Spirit so that I may be victorious in every battle.

I make this prayer in the strong name of Jesus Christ, with whom I am seated in the heavenly realms,

Amen.

CONCLUSION

In *Behold the Man*, we have tried to show how Jesus Christ represents a version of masculinity that is inspiring for Christian men today. Jesus Christ is truly the 'manly man'. He is not the hyper-masculine man of those who want him to be the 'ultimate fighting Jesus' with 'big biceps'. Nor is he the effeminate looking 'hippy Jesus' which the hyper-masculinity movement so trenchantly despises. Jesus Christ is rather a human being fully alive and in that respect he is an exhilarating model for both men and women. For Christians, true health arises from conforming oneself to the image of Christ rather than the image of Caesar — by which we mean the images of masculinity and femininity paraded on the stages of this world.

Of course the focus of *Behold the Man* has been masculinity rather than femininity. That is because both of us have fought to find our place as men in a church which is often under-represented by men. How are men to conduct themselves in such a feminized landscape? How can men be real men? What does it mean to be 'a real man' in Christ anyway? Is there a Biblical paradigm of manhood and masculinity which hasn't been sufficiently explored as yet and which might draw a generation of men magnetically into the church?

While Jesus Christ offers both men and women the truest example of what it means to be a new creation, we have proposed here that he also provides for men a redemptive image of manhood and masculinity which is subversive both in relation to the world's images and indeed to the macho images presented by some men in the church. Jesus Christ shows men what they can be in their inner world as well as in their outward conduct. He embodies a glorious vision for both manhood and masculinity.

Put succinctly, Jesus Christ revealed a manhood that was fashioned inwardly, not a masculinity carved outwardly. It was a manhood inscribed in the recesses of his heart, 'for out of the heart flow the issues of life' (Proverbs 4.23). Jesus Christ shows us that it is the condition of a man's heart that determines the masculinity he expresses. The heart of man's problem is the problem of man's heart. If a man's heart can be changed, then his conduct can be changed.

At the warp core of Jesus' manhood was his understanding of himself as 'Son.' He knew God was his *Abba*, his perfect, loving heavenly Father. He was in no doubt about this. From his baptism onwards, he lived in the grace-filled atmosphere of his acceptance as God's 'Beloved Son.' He addressed God as 'Dearest Father' or 'Papa' and did what he did not in order to be loved but simply because he was loved. His inner sense of his position as 'Son' was the engine that enabled and empowered him, with the help of the Holy Spirit, to fulfil the work the Father had entrusted to him. His outward conduct was therefore a product of his inner convictions. His manhood (his identity as Son) was the inspiration for his masculinity (the fulfilment of his God-given destiny).

For us, then, the key to being a manly man involves becoming a spiritual son by adoption, shedding over time the character traits that hampered us when we were spiritual orphans (such as rebellion, immorality, violence and inappropriate anger), and living out our sonship in a virtuous and productive life as manly men conformed to the image of Christ. This kind of masculinity is altogether different from the images provided by our culture. This kind of picture is much more counter-cultural and subversive, inspiring men to 'go the extra mile' rather than taking up weapons of destruction.

In this respect, Christ's version of manhood and masculinity is a manifestation of a different culture. It reflects the culture of heaven, or to use his phrase, 'the Kingdom of God.' This manhood and masculinity does not seek to express and extend itself through brute strength or force. That is the way of Empire not kingdom. Rather, Christ's revisionist expression of manhood and masculinity emphasizes being a loyal, royal, son, and that means self-sacrificial love and peaceful but authoritative resistance to the powers.

Mark writes:

'I remember going on holiday to Majorca about two years after I was ordained. There I made friends with three Scottish men in their twenties. They wanted to play tennis and needed an extra player so that they could enjoy doubles. They asked me to join them and I said yes.

For the next week we spent an hour or so every day playing tennis and getting to know each other.

Towards the end of the holiday I stayed up all night with them enjoying their company. They weren't Christians. They worshipped football (or what our American friends call 'soccer').

At about three o'clock in the morning one of them asked me what I did for a living. I told them I'd go and buy them a drink on the condition that they all three of them came up with their best guess.

The closest was 'undertaker!'

When I told them I was a Church of England Vicar they practically fell off their chairs. They couldn't believe that someone who was 'normal' and 'fun' could be ordained. It blew their preconceptions out of the water.

For the next three hours, until dawn, they one by one opened up to me about their lives — their wounds and their sins. They were totally honest and at times deeply moved. It was an indescribable honour and privilege to hear their stories.

Two of them left to go to bed.

This just left Steve — a broad shouldered and big muscled Rangers supporter built like a brick outhouse.

Before he left, he turned to me and said,

'Mark, I am not a church goer. But I do respect Jesus a lot.'

'Why?' I asked.

'Because he's the only man that would die for a **** like me,' he answered.

'He's the only real man who's ever lived,' he added, before shuffling off to bed.

That was nearly thirty years ago and I have never forgotten the conversation.'

Now here's the point of telling that story.

Steve did not have a picture of Jesus with biceps and an oozy when he thought about authentic masculinity. He had a picture of Jesus dying for him on a Roman cross.

Where that picture came from I have no idea. Maybe it was from his mother, or a Sunday school teacher, or a friend.

But that picture spoke to him deeply.

The crucified carpenter was for him the only real man he'd ever come across.

It was a suffering, peace-loving man not a triumphant, aggressive man that proved to be 'the manly man.'

Christ-like manhood and masculinity therefore form an extremely compelling model for men both outside and inside the church. This paradigm demands far more of men than simply shooting or shouting at those who oppress you. Put another way, it is much closer to the model provided by Dr Martin Luther King than to the on-screen supermen portrayed by Arnold Schwarzenegger. Christian men are called to be adopted sons who follow the example of the Son by nature. This means proclaiming and demonstrating the Gospel of peace. It means being self-sacrificial and Spirit-endued peacemakers because in that redemptive role Christian men reveal their true sonship and will one day receive the honour of being declared 'the sons of God' in the new heavens and the new earth.

The Roman image of manhood and masculinity is of course the furthest remove from this. The Emperor embodied what it meant to be a manly man in the time of the New Testament. This paradigm however was a paradigm forged on the anvil of imperialism. The paradigm provided by Jesus Christ is quite different. It is not an imperialistic model at all, and in this respect preachers need to be careful not to create a model of masculinity inspired more by an imperialistic impulse than by the Spirit of the Resurrected One. Christian men are not called to colonise the world flexing muscles and wielding weapons. They are called to serve the world not to dominate it — to a ministry of infiltration not of occupation.

This, then, is a very different kind of picture from the ones provided currently by the world and indeed the church. In many ways, men in the church seem to be calling other men to conform themselves to the image of Caesar more than the image of Christ. Theirs is a Christianised version of the nation-invading military man rather than the much tougher and more radical vision of the Christ-shaped man.

Our hope is that this book will help readers to 'behold the man' and in the process to 'become the man.'

Our prayer is that it will help men to conform to the image of Christ not Caesar.

John concludes:

'How do these findings relate to my personal ministry and leadership within the church where I serve? They have given me a profound understanding that as a Christian it is a non-negotiable necessity that I reveal Christ's image in me as a man. This has become a major pursuit for me.

One of the drivers for this is my longing to become a good example to other men. The apostle Paul said, 'imitate me, just as I also imitate Christ' (I Corinthians 11.1). I believe that the world is waiting to see authentic manhood and masculinity. Women are longing to know men who will love them as Christ loved the church and gave himself for her. Children are in desperate need of fathers who will reflect the image of their heavenly Father. Society as a whole needs leaders who reflect the image of integrity, righteousness, humility and selflessness which I believe originates in Jesus Christ, the most compassionate man in history.

I have come to realise that the search for authentic masculinity is one that can only truly be fulfilled in Jesus Christ. Manhood is derived from within, shaped by the Spirit of God through the Word of God.

My purpose as a minister and leader is to exemplify Christ's nature firstly in my relationship with my wife and children in my home, secondly in the church as I follow Christ's example empowered by the Holy Spirit.

Being a real man means being Christ-like.

Christ-likeness and true manhood are therefore synonymous, as indeed are Christ-likeness and being human.

Jesus Christ was a man and is forever a man, but the Canon of Scripture reveals that his life and nature are available for men and women to reveal. He is God and in his divinity he pours his life into all who believe in him, enabling them to reflect his image and his nature.

This is my mission, to bring those whom God has entrusted to me to the saving knowledge of Jesus Christ and echo the Westminster Catechism statement that the chief end of man is to 'glorify God and enjoy him forever.'

Bibliography

Books Consulted and Cited by John Triffitt and Dr Mark Stibbe

Augustus, Emperor: *Res Gestae Divi Augusti*. On-line English translation by Thomas Bushnell: all quotations taken from, http://classics.mit.edu/Augustus/deeds.html

Augustus, Emperor: *The Julian Marriage Laws*. On-line at http://www.unrv.com/government/julianmarriage.php

Bartkowski, J.P (2004) *The Promise Keepers: Servants, Soldiers and Godly Men:* Rutgers University Press

Cole, E. (1992) *Real Man:* Thomas Nelson.

Cole, E. (1982) *Maximized Manhood: A Guide to Family Survival:* Whitaker House

Cole, E. (1987) *Communication, Sex and Money:* Harrison House

Conway, C. (2008) *Behold the Man: Jesus and Greco-Roman Masculinity:* Oxford University Press

Covey, S. (2008) *The Speed of Trust:* Simon and Schuster Ltd.

Cowan, R. (2003) *The Roman Legionary: 58 BC—AD 69:* Osprey Publishing

Earle, R. (1989) *Word Meanings in the New Testament:* Baker Books, Grand Rapids

Elderidge, J. (2001) *Wild at Heart: Discovering the Secret of a Man's Soul:* Thomas Nelson

Everitt, A. (2007) *The First Emperor: Caesar Augustus and the Triumph of Rome:* John Murray

Foucault, M. (1990) *The History of Sexuality Volume 1:* An Introduction: Vintage Books

Faludi, S. (1999) *Stiffed: The Betrayal of the American Man:* William Morrow and Company

Gilmore, D. (1990) *Manhood in the Making: Cultural Concepts of Masculinity:* Yale University Press

Hybels, B. (2002) *Courageous Leadership:* Zondervan, Grand Rapids

Juvenal, *Satires.* 10:356 *(for mens sana in corpora sano aphorism).*

Lasch, C. (1980) *The Culture of Narcissism:* London, Abacus

Lincoln, A. (1990) *Ephesians. Word Biblical Commentary:* Volume 42

Livy, *The History of Rome,* Vol.1 (translation, Canon Roberts. Edition: Everyman's Library, J.M. Dent and Sons (London); E.P. Dutton and Co. (New York, 1912). For the story of Cincinnatus: http://courses.cvcc.vccs.edu/ history_mcgee/courses/his101/Source%20Documents/wc1d11.htm

Macaulay, Lord Thomas Babington (1800-1859), *Horatius poem:* http://ancienthistory.about.com/library/bl/bl_horatiuspoem.htm

McCloughry, R. (1992) *Men and Masculinity, from power to love:* Hodder and Stroughton

McDonnell, M. (2006) *Roman Manliness, Virtus and the Roman Republic:* Cambridge University Press.

McGrath, A. (2011) *Christian Theology: An Introduction:* Blackwell Publishers

McKnight, Scott and Modica. (2013) *Joseph, Jesus is Lord, Caesar is not.* Evaluating Empire in New Testament Studies:IVP Academic

Milne, B. (1982) *Know the Truth: A Handbook of Christian Belief:* InterVarsity Press

Moore, S. and Anderson, J.C. (2003) *New Testament Masculinities:* Society of Bible

Mosse, G.L. (1996) *The Image of Man: The Creation of Modern Masculinity:* Oxford University Press

Philo, *On the Embassy to Gaius:* http://www.earlychristianwritings.com/yonge/book40.html

Pleck, J.H. (1981) *The Myth of Masculinity:* MIT Press Cambridge

Peterson, E. (2006) *Eat this Book:* Hodder & Stoughton

Polybius: *The Histories, Book 6:* http://penelope.uchicago.edu/Thayer/E/Roman/Texts/Polybius/6*.html

Prince, D. (2000) *Husbands and Fathers: Rediscover the Creator's Purpose for Men:* Sovereign World Ltd

Sanders, E.P. (1992) *Judaism Practice and Belief 63-66 CE:* Trinity Press International.

Stott, J. (1991) *The Glory and the Shame:* Third Way

Suetonius, *The life of Nero.* http://lexundria.com/suet_nero/26-32/r

Suetonius, *The Lives of the Twelve Caesars* http://www.gutenberg.org/files/6400/6400-h/6400-h.htm

Swinton, J & Mowat, H (2006) *Practical Theology and Qualitative Research:* SCM Press

The Holy Bible (1996) *New King James Version:* Broadman and Holman Publishers

Tozer, A.W. (2010) *Discovering the Presence of God:* Regal Gospel Light

Tozer, A.W (1987) *Knowledge of the Holy:* Kingsway

Wink, W. (2003) *Jesus and Nonviolence: A Third Way:* Augsburg Fortress

Data & Statistics:

Offender Management Statistics Quarterly Bulletin

https://www.gov.uk/government/uploads/system/uploads/attachment_data/file/192314/omsq-q4-oct-dec-2012__2_.pdf

http://www.parliament.uk/briefing-papers/SN04334.pdfs

http://www.amnesty.org.uk/violence-against-women#.VFNrB1efOo0

http://www.parliament.uk/briefingpapers/commons/lib/research/briefings/snsg-04334.pdf

Walby, S. & Allen, J. *Domestic violence, sexual assault and stalking:* Findings from the British Crime Survey. Home Office. London. (from 'Statistics on Domestic Violence':www.womensaid.org.uk)

HM Government *Cross-government Action Plan on Sexual Violence and Abuse.* Home Office. London(from 'Statistics on Domestic Violence':www.womensaid.org.uk)

Amnesty UK *Sexual Assault Research.* Amnesty. London. (from 'Statistics on Domestic Violence': www.womensaid.org.uk)

Responding to Domestic Abuse. DH. London. (from 'Statistics on Domestic Violence': www.womensaid.org.uk)

Dodd, T. et al (2004) Crime in England and Wales 2003-2004. Home Office. London (from 'Statistics on Domestic Violence': www.womensaid.org.uk)

Forced Marriage: A Wrong not a Right, Home Office and Foreign & Commonwealth Office, 2005 (from 'Statistics on Domestic Violence': www. womensaid.org.uk)

Walby, S. The Cost of Domestic Violence (from 'Statistics on Domestic Violence': www.womensaid.org.uk)

Testimonies:

Chris Keeble: Falklands Testimony, taken from the article, 'Falklands Revisited: Officer Recalls How Prayer led to Peace': http://www.ncregister. com/site/article/falklands_revisited_officer_recalls_how_prayer_led_to_ peace/

Horatius Cocles, Roman soldier and hero: Taken from Livy's, *History of Rome from its foundation* 2.10; (translation by Rev Canon Roberts). On line version at http://www.livius.org/ho-hz/horatius/cocles.html

The Forty Martyrs of Sabaste: taken originally from St. Basil's Homily 20.1.

Centurion Marcellus: Taken from Vol. III of *The Lives or the Fathers, Martyrs and Other Principal Saints* by the Rev. Alban Butler.

Canon Andrew White: http://www.ft.com/cms/s/2/e3d1e822-e3f9-11e2-91a3-00144feabdc0.html#axzz3HSRTTI1G

Made in the USA
Columbia, SC
05 March 2019